AROUND IRELAND WITH A PAN

D1382523

First published in 2004 by Liberties Press
51 Stephens Road | Inchicore | Dublin 8 | Ireland
www.libertiespress.com | info@libertiespress.com
Editorial: +353 (1) 402 0805 | sean@libertiespress.com
Sales and marketing: +353 (1) 453 4363 | peter@libertiespress.com

Trade enquiries to CMD Distribution
55A Spruce Avenue | Stillorgan Industrial Park | Blackrock | County Dublin
Tel: +353 (1) 294 2560
Fax: +353 (1) 294 2564

Copyright Éamonn Ó Catháin, 2004

ISBN 0-9545335-3-4

2 4 6 8 10 9 7 5 3 1

A CIP record for this title is available from the British Library

Cover design by Liam Furlong at space.ie
Author photographs by Peter Houlihan
Landscape photograph by Harry Weir Photography
Illustrations by Dermot Hall

Printed in Ireland by Colour Books
Unit 105 | Baldoyle Industrial Estate | Dublin 13

Around Ireland with a Pan
Food, Tales and Recipes

Éamonn Ó Catháin

LIB
ERT
IES

To my mother and father
who for years have had to put up with me
banging on about food

ACKNOWLEDGEMENTS

I would like to thank all the chefs who contributed recipes to this book, the staff in various restaurants around the country who put up with my nocturnal visits and fruity conversation, the publishers for putting this out there, the editor for making sense of it, Annette for keeping my spirits up, and Master Darach Ó Catháin for his instant criticisms of much of the food.

CONTENTS

MUNSTER

CONNACHT

FOREWORD

I've known about Éamonn Ó Catháin almost since I first returned
to Northern Ireland, more than fifteen years ago. My first restaurant had begun to draw reviews from the media. Secretly I hoped
I would have the edge over the local competition because I had just
returned from a two-and-a-half-year stint in the Napa Valley,
California, a cook's paradise. I was constantly being caught out,
however.

One of the most influential of these early 'critiques' was a pro-
file of five Irish chefs, done in the Aer Lingus in-flight magazine
Cara, a kind of 'low-down on the latest' type of thing. The article
had repercussions for years: numerous customers would mention
it as the reason they decided to visit, the odd producer would call
to offer me something special. Needless to say, I was very proud
to have appeared beside these famous Irish chefs – and yes, one of
them was Éamonn.

It was my first introduction to this chef Éamonn O'whatever-
you-call-him, and I was curious. He looked like a confident, slightly scruffy and rather bohemian type of guy. What stood out in his
'brief' was his obvious love of food, and his funky cooking style.
No wonder that his place in Dublin, Shay Beano, was one of the
hottest little restaurants on the map.

My first visit to Shay Beano only confirmed Éamonn's style
and character. My wife and I had popped in on the off chance of
getting a table, hoping to grab an early bite before returning home
to Belfast. The restaurant wasn't even open for the night yet, but
I remember the Irish hospitality. 'You want a quick bite?' 'Sure,
come on in.' 'No, no trouble at all. Have a seat.'

Éamonn was striking what is now a familiar pose, sitting at the
back of the restaurant, chair tilted back, chatting with a couple of
friends over a bottle of red wine. I can still taste that delicious rustic salad of roast rabbit with olives, and Jeanne had a perfect little
leek-and-Gruyère tart with mixed baby greens. It was simple yet
discerning stuff.

Over the years, our friendship has grown in the manner of

friendships between busy chefs. We usually bump into each other in restaurants. 'Ach, Eamonn, how ya doing? Had any good meals lately?' 'What, just back from France? Again? You lucky sod!' And so on, always with another tale to be told.

I love to see Éamonn at our bar in Cayenne, sharing a bottle of wine and a few starters with friends or colleagues. I love that he understands our food and what we are trying to do. He's one of our favourite and most welcome customers.

Imagine then when the chance for Éamonn to head off round Ireland talking food to its restaurateurs and producers, and eating all along the way as well, pops up. A great job offer, to be sure, but who could really bring it alive? Yep, none other. It seems to me that Éamonn gets a lot of the good jobs.

Reading his stories, there's no doubt that he's led an adventurous and fascinating life. But he also has a unique gift of the gab, and, for a chef, a real way with the pen (or keyboard!). That's his charm. His is an easygoing, humorous style that personifies and captures the spirit of particular characters and then connects them to some wonderful dish. Derryman Dermot Doherty helped Éamonn to discover . . . *kleftico!* Of course! Through Dermot's Cypriot brother-in-law! I'm still not sure whether Éamonn's making some of it up, but who cares. There are many delicious-looking recipes in these stories, from the native to, well, the African Congo, no less. Some very humble stuff, and some very upbeat and posh French 'cuisine'. We even get the recipe for brochette of shark that was a favourite of Mark Knopfler and the boys from U2.

The journey this book travels, over the fields and into the frying pans of the Emerald Isle, will fit snugly yet comfortably on my crowded cookbook shelves. I'm sure it will wink at me on occasion, catching my eye and promising to take me for a witty and memorable walk across my home territories, discussing favourite topics, and never failing to capture my spirit and entertain me for hours. Almost as pleasurable as sitting with Éamonn himself, with a bottle of red wine and a few shared plates.

Paul Rankin, June 2004

AUTHOR'S INTRODUCTION

Why would anyone in their right mind want to begin a meal in a restaurant with a first course of a glass of orange juice? Yet that was the way it used to be in Ireland in the seventies.

Every menu idea that came down to us from Continental Europe was watered down and rendered cheaper to produce. Take the classic 'chef's chicken-liver pate with toast', based on seared foie gras with brioche. This dullard of a starter was garnished not-at-all-tantalisingly with limp lettuce, tired tomato and the dreaded cucumber – and never served with enough toast. How did it come to be that something that was created with parsimony in mind could skimp on the toast and not on the pâté?

This was how things were: chicken Maryland, resplendent with its ring of tinned pineapple and cherry, prawn cocktail with a sickly-sweet sauce, half a roast duck falling so perfectly off the bone it must have been deep-fried after having the bejaysus boiled out of it. It was a time of pavlova and Black Forest gateau, which, like the foie gras, had been changed beyond recognition. And Black Forest gateau then metamorphosed into tiramisu. Poor tiramisu! I once ate in a café that served fifty outstanding varieties of this pick-me-up in downtown Turin, each one better than the one before. In Ireland, we did away with the mascarpone and replaced it with Philadelphia, and the espresso-soaked coffee was increasingly laced with instant coffee instead.

So eventually we Irish decided to learn how to cook, and things changed dramatically for the better. It became headline news in Dublin newspapers when the likes of Patrick Guilbaud praised our young men and women chefs and said that they were actually getting quite good. Until then, we had been in awe of French chefs; the suggestion that ours could not only take them on but beat them at international level was both astonishing and a matter of pride.

But are our modern menus so great? Chiches abound, and classic dishes have been overworked beyond endurance. Take Thai fish cakes: all of Ireland's restaurateurs seemingly discovered, at exactly the same time, that they could use up all their fishy bits and trimmings, bang in any auld Oriental spices, and the punters would love it. Thai food for dummies.

Likewise, confit of duck. Restaurants have realised that this dependable French perennial is cheap to buy and cheap to produce, presents no difficulties as to well-done, medium or rare, and has a longer shelf life than most products. (It's very name, 'confit', means 'preserved'.) And so we offer it up regardless of the type of restaurant, play with it, and even – horrors! – Asian-ise it. And how about mashed potato? Joel Robuchon does something witty with a few potatoes in his three-star restaurant in Paris, and six years later mash is on every table in Ireland. Basil mash, mustard mash, Meaux-mustard mash, garlic mash, roast-garlic mash, Thai-bloody-fish-cake mash.

Do I paint a grim picture? Only in order to highlight our increasing maturity now that we've got over our foodie puberty. Ireland, in common with many other gastronomically challenged parts of Europe, is enjoying a culinary renaissance: a huge change in attitudes to food and our cooking of it. And not before time. The Ireland of many years ago, as recounted by Amhlaoibh Ó Suilleabháin in his diary *Cinn Lae Amhlaoibh*, ate not just well but interestingly, with both intricate native dishes (feasts always included both a hefty fish course, with salmon being prized, and a serious meat course) and drinks such as whiskey-and-milk *psaltair*.

Today we have a modern Irish cuisine, based on native ingredients and using pan-European techniques: a trend evidenced by our blossoming restaurant culture. And unlike the rest of Europe, our brilliant young chefs have gone one better and developed some of the most innovative and creative menus you can find anywhere. I am constantly surprised and thrilled to find genuinely interesting and challenging dishes the length and breadth of this country, the like of which you will not see anywhere else. If you walk the streets of Dublin and Cork, you will be gladdened by menus no two of which are alike. Try doing the same in Paris.

In time, such is the extent of Irish chefs' creativity, diners' exploration of new tastes, and the hard work on the part of producers, growers and farmers, Ireland could develop a genuine regional gastronomy. Just drop the confit of duck, will yiz, lads?

10

ULSTER

DONEGAL

Like many a Belfast boy before me, I was informed at the age of eleven that I was 'going to the Gaeltacht' for a month. It was information that filled me with dread, for despite a lifelong familiarity with the Irish language, I had never heard of this 'Gaeltacht' or anyone who might live in it. But most of all, I didn't want to leave home at all.

I cried for all three weeks that I spent in Gaoth Dobhair: I was a wee city-slicker adrift in a rural hell. They had real cows, for God's sake, cocks that went *'mac na h-óighe slán'* ('cock-a-doodle-doo') every bloody morning at Irish time, Paris time and New York time, milk that was warm with things floating on top, strange-tasting bread that sure wasn't white, and little that was recognisable from home. Like the France that I was to discover a few years later, I couldn't wait to get out of it; just like France, as soon as I was home, I couldn't wait to return.

That first time took an awful lot of adjusting to, but it wasn't all bad. For one thing, there were chip shops serving *'sceallogai preátaí'*. We sneaked out to these places most nights to fill our young tums, which were starved of Belfast industrial food. This was a fine arrangement until one night we all got caught by our *bean a' toighe* (the woman of the house), who laid into us, demanding to know what was wrong with her food. I learned more adult Irish in that five-minute rant than in the next five years. There was nothing wrong with her food at all, of course, and it is to this budding gourmet's shame that I had such a negative reaction to what was, after all, real food.

Other delights which saved our bacon, so to speak, included Cadbury Ireland, with its unsuspected and myriad confections, which were simply not available in the six counties. Money and postal orders from home were frittered away on every bar of chocolate available – usually in the one day. This was washed down by that unique and ubiquitous Donegal drink, the blessed banana lemonade. Banana lemonade – try explaining that to British visitors – was simply unknown beyond the borders of

Donegal. It must have been the most synthetic soft drink ever but, as I was convinced it was really made from bananas, for me it has remained ever since the taste of holidays, reminding me of the *céilídh mhór* – bringing to mind the memory of dozens of tiny Sally O'Briens 'and the way they might look at you'. (This was the catchphrase from a hugely successful Harp ad run throughout Ireland in the early 1980s. The young men of Ireland all fell in love with the enigmatic Sally O'Brien – who turned out, in real life, to be English.) No doubt these days I would find this particular beverage positively ghastly.

They did have chickens, though – loads of them. And we slickers, eager to exploit the ways of the country, quickly found the method of dispatching them. It was learned early on that the one meal we did care for was roast chicken – and also that the chickens least likely to make it to adulthood were those that consumed their own eggs. That was our cue: every other day we fired an egg or two at the fattest bird, secure in the knowledge that it would rush towards the egg and dip its beak in the raw yolk. One of us would then fetch the *fear a' toighe* (the man of the house) and grass up the poor bird with a well-rehearsed *'Dearc ar an tsicín seo ag ithe an uibh'* ('Look at this chicken eating the egg') – and, hey presto, roast chicken for us the next day. Hard men that we were, we probably even offered to wring its neck for him. Oh, the shame.

In the following summer – of 1968 – though, I just couldn't wait to go back to the Gaeltacht, and a glorious sun shone non-stop for the two months I was there. I was now in love with Donegal forever. I learned to appreciate the food and the ceaseless entreaties to eat *tuilleadh preátaí* (more potatoes) and to speak up and say *'Go rabh mo dhotháin agam'* ('I've had my fill'). I stayed in all the main Gaeltacht villages – Falcarragh, Derrybeg, Rannafast and so on – and, just like a local, learned to wave at every car that drove past. Eventually I went up one week of my own accord, with a mate from Belfast. I found a hen house – a *hen house* – to live in for a week and cooked food on fragrant turf fires in its entrance. It seemed to me that I was a real pioneer, living off the fat of the land, even though what I was 'cooking' was probably tins of soup and tins of beans and tins of ravioli – which was my favourite, once upon a time. In addition, we accepted the odd pot of real soup, and of course a bowl of *preátaí bruite* (boiled pota-toes) from the kindest people you could hope to meet anywhere. The bowl had been humped across fields of soaking-wet turf by a smiling urchin sent by her mother, who had taken pity on these two children who had elected to live in a hen house for a week. Is it any wonder that Belfast people have a reputation for being quite mad?

The only problem was that I didn't realise that my hen house was actually made from turf: within thirty-six hours I had burnt it down with my early attempts at cooking. We hid from our kind mashed-potato suppliers for at least four days, until we were told by fellow rogues that 'they were glad that that eyesore' had final-ly been removed from the landscape. We then gratefully reinte-grated ourselves into society.

*

Donegal in those days was never known for its food. Despite the advent of fine seafood restaurants into other *Gaeltachtaí* such as Connemara, where French, Italian and German tourists abound-ed, somehow Donegal managed to escape this revolution, no doubt hampered by the legions of northerners who flood into it all year round, demanding not good food but *ceol, caint agus craic* (music, conversation and craic). Although matters have improved, things are not that different these days: on the rise near Derrybeg there are so many fast-food joints that the area is known by the locals as 'Vinegar Hill' – which I must say is rather witty. Indeed, where a search on the Internet will reveal the existence of *www.dun-na-ngall.com*, it is amazing – if not suprising – to note that, of the site's twenty-two sub-pages, not one is dedicated to eat-ing out, restaurants or food. A recent visit to Gaoth Dobhair, however, revealed a plethora of acceptable-if-not-splendid restau-rants and bistros unheard of in my day – and revelling in one of the finest vistas in Ireland.

By far the most surprising thing in terms of food in Donegal is the existence of a superb restaurant several miles from Bunbeg in the village of Annagry known as Danny Minnies: it is an oasis of civilisation in the midst of the gorgeous wilderness. Open only from April to October, it is a sheer pleasure, by virtue of its sumptuous turf fires and sumptuous food: in addition to classic fine steaks it also offers sublime seafood. The antique furnishings and oak panelling belie the fact that one is still in the heart of the Rosses of Donegal. Danny Minnies is an established addition to the scene and one can only hope that it inspires many imitators.

Is mithid go bhfuil a leithid ann faoi dheireadh i Rosaibh Thír Chonaill agus mar sin mo bhuíochas agus mo chomhghairdeachas do mhuintir Uí Dhomhnaill as Anagaire gur leofa an tsár-bhialann seo. Go deimhin, bíonn fear de chuid na clainne, mar atá Brian Ó Domhnaill, ag cócaireacht ann o am go chéile nuair nach bhfuil sé le feiceáil ar an teilifís ar TG4 lena chuid cláracha bidh macasamhail Nuabhia Gaelach.

Who can make mention of Donegal without referring to wee Daniel? Those visiting 'the shrine', and therefore the village of Kincasslagh, would be well advised to visit Iggy's Pub, run by Iggy and Anne Murray. While the pub serves food only during the tourist season, its seafood delights are legendary, and paragons of simplicity.

East Donegal is considerably better served by restaurants, most notable of which is Kealy's Seafood Bar in the small fishing port of Greencastle. Kealy's is justly renowned for its seafood, which all comes fresh from the harbour. This restaurant's reputation extends far beyond the shores of Lough Foyle, on which it is perched: it numbers John Hume among its many patrons and is a mecca for fish- and seafood-lovers. Not to be missed either is Kee's Hotel in Stranorlar, which houses two restaurants: the Old Gallery, for casual dining, and the Looking Glass, where Ulster meets France under the inspired hand of chef Franck Pasquier.

Above all, Donegal is justly famous for its scenery, for its magnificent, kind and friendly people, and for its *teangaidh mhaith ghaedhilge* (beautiful Irish language). It was on a recent visit that I met the two sisters Ní Ghiolla Bhríde, unsung custodians of an oral tradition. I spent several splendid hours in their company and had the pleasure of cooking two dishes for them: a quiche made from nettles that grew around their house, and a West Indian *calalou*, filled with fresh fish from Killybegs in south Donegal. These two simple recipes are given below.

PÍÓG NA GCOL FAIDH
– NETTLE QUICHE

Kitty Ní Ghiolla Bhríde told me all about the famine *(an droch-shaol)* in Gaoth Dobhair and environs and the foods that were eaten then: the cornmeal that featured in many a story by the Rannafast writer Maire (Seamas Ó Grianna) and the edible sea-weeds to be found down by the strand.

It seemed only fitting that I should try and make something with whatever I could find to hand. Her garden was full of nettles. That was it! We would make a quiche with them. Kitty reminded me of the local expression for them – *col faidh* – hence the title.

250g plain flour
125g salted butter
Glass of salted water
7 eggs
Salt, pepper and nutmeg
200ml cream
50ml milk
Nettles
150g Gruyère cheese, grated

for the pastry:
Incorporate the butter gradually into the flour until you achieve a sandy consistency. Then add one whole egg, mix that in and add water a little at a time to bind the mixture. Form a ball of dough, then roll it in a little flour and put in the fridge.

for the filling:
Beat the remaining six eggs together as for an omelette, then add the cream and milk (to make the quiche lighter). Season with salt and pepper, grate a little nutmeg into the mixture and add the grat-ed Gruyère.

Wash the nettles (using gloves). Blanch them by plunging them into boiling water. After only a few seconds, remove the nettles

17

and refresh them under cold running water. Place the leaves on a chopping board and, holding them tightly, chop them finely with a sharp knife.

Roll out the pastry, place in a buttered tart ring and spread the chopped nettles over the base. Pour the mix over this, covering the nettles (to ensure they will not burn). Finally, grate some more nutmeg over the top and place in a preheated hot oven for around fifteen to twenty minutes, until golden-brown. (Turn the quiche around every five minutes so that the heat is distributed evenly.) When the quiche has risen and is browned on top and fully cooked, remove it from the oven, and from the ring. Serve immediately.

I love the food of the West Indies, a largely seasonal cuisine, full of exciting, spicy flavours, where freshness is of paramount importance. Of all the islands, I love best the cuisine of Martinique and Guadeloupe, the French West Indies, where local produce and know-how is happily married to French techniques and trends, resulting in a dynamic national cuisine.

Calalou is one of the dishes that is common to all the islands, be they French, English, Dutch, Spanish, Creole or Papiamento-speaking: a true pan-Caribbean dish. Despite what I've written above, it is the version eaten in Trinidad that I have the fondest memories of, partly perhaps because I spent more time there than anywhere else, but mainly because it was scrumptious: more of a stew there than a soup (as on the other islands). The finest one that I ate was down by Pigeon Point in Tobago at lunchtime. It was sold at a roadside stall and eaten without ceremony on some steps.

So loved is this dish that I can think of a dozen or more calypsos that sing its praises. In fact, I know of no other music in the world which goes on about food as much as the soca of Trinidad and Tobago: every ingredient below has been mentioned in one or other soca over the years.

I never thought that one day I would end up cooking this dish for two lovely Donegal women in glorious sunshine up the road from Na Doirí Beaga. Since I did, I worked out which ingredients I could replace, since not all of them are available in this country. Here is the recipe, a hybrid of Trinidad, Martinique and Irish techniques – and a great dish.

A bunch of *dasheen* leaves, also known as '*calalou* bush'
    (available from some Chinese supermarkets; if it is not
    obtainable, replace with spinach)
A dozen okra ('ladies' fingers'), sliced lengthways
400g crabmeat
1 pig tail, chopped
    (this is traditionally used throughout the islands; lardons
    or smoked bacon pieces will work just as well)

1 bunch of chives
1 hot red pepper
1 clove of garlic, crushed and chopped
Chopped celery leaves
1 bunch of thyme
1 bunch of parsley
Juice of one lime (or 2 tablespoons of white-wine vinegar)

Serves 4

Finely chop the parsley with the celery leaves. Sauté the pig tail or bacon in the bottom of a large pot with a little oil. When the meat has browned, add a litre of water and the *dasheen* leaves or spinach. Then add the okra, garlic, chives, thyme and hot pepper whole. Bring to the boil, then add the crab. Leave to simmer for one hour.

Season with salt and pepper to taste; add the vinegar or lime juice. I like to grate the lime zest over the calalou at the end. If you continue to let the dish reduce, it will thicken and become more like a stew; otherwise, you can take it off the heat after an hour or so and serve as a soup. *Calalou* can be served with rice. Then, as they say in those parts: 'Come drink up we *calalou.*'

FERMANAGH

Many's the time that I have driven (nay, been chauffered, if truth be told) to Donegal, passing through County Fermanagh and towns such as Enniskillen on the way: one could certainly be forgiven for thinking that there isn't too much going on there food-wise. The county of Fermanagh is exquisite from a scenic point of view, the beautiful lakes giving Killarney a fair old run for their money, but restaurants appear scarce, while shopfronts and façades are quite dour in appearance. Older editions of John McKenna's *Bridgestone Irish Food Guide* simply omitted the county.

Fermanagh is of course famous for its fishing, a fact known to legions of foreign tourists – Germans, for the most part. Its lakes abound in wild salmon and trout, not to mention birds and wild flowers. However, I is no fisherman, me. Don't ask me nuttin' about fishing, for I have no clue. I cook fish and roast birds. (Oh, and I stuffed wild flowers with fish mousses during the worst excesses of nouvelle cuisine in the 1980s.) It's not that I don't care about where things come from: I do, but for me food is to be eaten and relished, not photographed and anguished over.

Lough Melvin is the one to go for if you fish. This is a huge lake that recognises no border between the north of Ireland and the 'other side' – ridiculously described as the 'south' – and is home to no fewer than five varieties of trout, including the ferox, brown trout, sea trout, sonaghan and gillaroo. The sonaghan, which is unique to the lake, is described by authorities as exquisite and even extraordinary. It needs no more cooking than to be either poached or grilled, with just melted butter as an accompanying sauce. I'm reliably informed that the sonaghan is the fish to have for breakfast, though this, I confess, is beyond my ken as I simply cannot contemplate fish for breakfast, no matter how subtle, unique or delicious it is.

Fish aside, the region harbours a zealot – a food zealot, I hasten to point out. Pat O'Doherty is a butcher by trade and an environmental scientist by profession: he has brought many of the concerns and sensitivities of the latter to the quality control of the former. Pat, whose shop is in the town of Enniskillen, is now rightly famous for his main product, 'black bacon' (a trademarked product). Ask Pat a question about his bacon – his baby – and you will receive a passionate tirade about bacon, Ireland, the cooking of local produce and the development of an Irish cuisine. He is a man with a mission – and pride and know-how to match.

Pat recalls how the supermarket trends of the seventies and eighties changed Irish people's style of life and the quality of the products that we eat. In his opinion, Irish bacon died a death in the seventies, due to the supermarkets. Not content with letting things be – and admitting to being embarrassed by the products that he himself was selling as Irish bacon – five years ago he decided to do something about it and went straight to the source: the older people, farmers and pig breeders who could recall the old style and flavours of bacon and the methods that were used to make it. He used the information he collated, and then experimented, refined and honed the product: the resulting meat, black bacon, uses older methods of production in a hygienic, modern manner, with strict controls applicable to the levels of salt and nitrates in the meat.

Pat explains that, while nitrites and nitrates are preservatives, they change the colour of the bacon from grey to pink. As a result, it was only as recently as November 2003 that he dared to put a completely nitrite- and E-number-free bacon on the market, when he launched it at a food fair in London. Customers are not used to seeing bacon with a colour such as this, and so there must be a process of re-education before nitrates can be removed completely from the entire range. Nonetheless, Pat is convinced that his work represents a major breakthrough in bacon production.

Pat's black bacon is now an award-winning product – as are his sausages and even his burgers – and he is justly proud of it. The appellation 'black' has nothing to do with Guinness, as many suppose, but relates to the type of doner pig involved, the black pig. Pat uses three types of this pig: the saddleback, the Wessex and, his favourite, the Tamworth, which, being an excellent outdoor forager, is ideally suited to Irish woodland, as well as providing superb meat.

As business at Pat's butcher's shop has snowballed, supermarkets have been, as he put it, 'torturing him' for the product, even phoning him on his mobile as early as 7 AM and queuing at his door. Pat is not for turning, however. He is more than happy with black bacon as a niche product, selling it directly to restaurants and foodie outlets, including the famous Harrod's food halls in London, and Brussels, where it is doing very well. In fact, the magnificent chef Derry Clarke recently cooked black bacon at the Ballygowan/Irish Food Writers Guild Awards in his Michelin-starred Dublin restaurant, L'Écrivain.

Now several other black-bacon products have joined the range, including oak-smoked and nitrate-free varieties. Pat wanted to offer an item from this range as a gift to Harrod's owner Mohammed al-Fayed but realised that it would not be the thing to give a pork product to someone of the Muslim faith. As a result, another product was created: oak-smoked Fermanagh lamb. Even the title is causing me to salivate: it is all I can do not to quit this keyboard and beat a retreat to Enniskillen to sample it.

On that note, where better to taste this lamb than one of the best restaurants in the area: Dermot Magee's Oscar's restaurant (named after Oscar Wilde, one of the many giants of Irish literature who was schooled in the area, at the Portora Royal School). Oscar's is situated in a beautiful building in the town of Enniskillen, and Dermot himself is a thoroughly affable and helpful sort who cooks local products with verve. He serves trout and salmon, including gillaroo and sonaghan (when available), not to mention the subtle treat of a black-bacon bruschetta. Indeed both Dermot and Pat put their heads together a few years back when products such as black bacon were being refined to promote the region's produce through local dishes in restaurants – and Dermot has responded with such a dish for the smoked Fermanagh lamb with a simple redcurrant jus and onion mash.

More information about O'Doherty's butchers and its products can be found at *www.blackbacon.com*. Pat has kindly donated the following two recipes from the website's excellent 'cookbook' page.

for the pasta:
500g plain flour
2 eggs (beaten with 100ml water)

for the ravioli filling:
25g butter
2 shallots, finely chopped
8 thin slices of streaky bacon,
    cut into strips and fried until crisp
200g wild mushrooms (e.g. ceps, morels or chanterelles),
    roughly chopped
1 skinless chicken breast (puréed with 1 egg white and 100ml
    double cream)
200g cooked spinach
250ml beef stock, reduced to sauce consistency
Flat-leaf parsley, chopped

Serves 4

Place the flour in a large mound on the work surface. Make a well
in the middle and pour in the egg mixture, keeping a little aside.
Mix with a fork, starting in the middle and working your way
out. Knead for ten minutes until elastic, then chill.

Sweat the shallot in the butter until translucent. Turn up the heat
and add the mushrooms, tossing in the pan until cooked. Season
and add the parsley and bacon. Fold the mushroom mixture into
the puréed chicken. Roll the pasta as thinly as possible, preferably
using a pasta machine, and cut into eight 12cm squares. Place a
large spoonful of filling onto the centre of four squares of pasta.
Moisten the edges of the pasta squares with the remaining egg mixture and place the other four pasta squares on top, pushing down
the edges to seal firmly.

Cook the ravioli in boiling salted water for approximately six minutes. Drain and keep warm. Heat the spinach and sauce. Put the spinach in the centre of each plate, place the ravioli on top and spoon around the sauce. This makes an excellent starter.

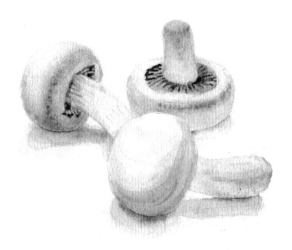

MONKFISH WRAPPED IN SPINACH AND BLACK BACON

4 six- to eight-ounce monkfish fillets, skinned
1lb cooked spinach
20 thin slices of dried bacon
1 savoy cabbage, shredded and cooked
250g mashed potato
White-wine vinegar
White wine
Butter

Serves 4

Lay four large squares of clingfilm on the work surface. Cover with most of the bacon, then with spinach, and place one piece of seasoned monkfish on each square. Wrap each mound of food tightly and tie the ends of the clingfilm. Leave to firm up in the fridge for at least an hour. Add the cabbage and the remaining bacon (chopped into strips) to the hot mashed potato and keep warm. Remove the clingfilm from the monkfish and cook the parcels in a little hot oil to crisp the bacon. Finish in the oven for five to ten minutes, depending on the thickness of the fish. Carve each parcel into six slices and serve with the potatoes and a light butter sauce. (Over a high heat, add a little white wine, a few drops of white-wine vinegar and several cubes of butter to the cooking juices).

TYRONE

When I was a wee boy, the only thing that seemed to come from Tyrone was a sausage – from Cookstown. No doubt I should have been aware of some great tradition of Gaelic football, but in my world the result was always: Food 1, Sport 0. I can still remember the ads on TV, punctuated by the big Rediffusion star from London, of a very sheepish George Best smiling at a pronged sausage with, I'm sure, a ditsy blonde in the background, while he mouthed the supremely witty line: 'Cookstown are the Best family sausages.' George was from East Belfast.

Tyrone is a place of wild beauty, full of bog and Sperrins. It has museums devoted to ancient Ireland and emigration to North America, and of course the county is dotted with standing stones and high crosses. But despite the building of a motorway to Dungannon, sleepy Tyrone hasn't changed much. In many ways, this is obviously 'a good thing', but the food revolution in Ireland has yet to penetrate. And why should it? We don't have a food culture in the same way that France, Spain or Italy has.

I've said it, so I'd better explain myself before I'm taken to task. We do have a fledgling food culture, and undeniably a thriving restaurant culture, but we have yet to make much headway as regards the food we eat at home. Not possessing a national cuisine – oh, we have a few potato-based dishes, Irish stew, coddle, champ and 'tattie bread', but that does not a cuisine make – we have pilfered from the entire world.

This makes for great fun when eating out, but it also makes for a 'magpie' cuisine in restaurants, where a dish can often cross-reference Japan, Morocco and Provence, all on the same plate (who's up for a tempura of ratatouille?). There's no great surprise in this: Ireland is moving ever forward in its pursuit of great food, and such extremes of poor judgement are disappearing rapidly as our knowledge and confidence mature.

Still, the sight of our young people, young boys especially, queuing at bus stops armed to the elbows with not one but several kinds of chocolate bars (and bad chocolate at that), plus two kinds of crisps, all washed down with a sugar-based carbonated drink, is a frightening one in these days of childhood obesity.

It also means that young palates are pampered with facile and unharmonious tastes: people think nothing of putting a salty crisp in their mouths followed by sweet chocolate. This continues in adulthood: how anyone can cheerfully swallow smoked kipper and wash it down with hot, sweet tea (or worse, coffee) with milk in it makes me shudder. Likewise, the poor habits of childhood and the chocolate-bar culture allow that some people will cheerfully wolf down a hearty, heavy fry and think nothing of drinking hot chocolate with it.

Of course, the price of food in Ireland has a lot to do with this situation: food is dear, and restaurants can be stupidly expensive, rarely offering real value for money. Mind you, Dublin has many more cheap-and-cheerful but good establishments than Belfast, despite the perceived wisdom that everything is cheaper in the north. Even in a decent establishment where the price for a meal for two might be exactly the same in both cities, Dublin will often score more highly because the quality of the ingredients may be better, the inventiveness superior, and the choice of wine on offer light years ahead. Wine-drinking has always been taken far more seriously in the twenty-six counties than in the northern six. Who could ever forget the insipid TV slots for 'Mundies Silver Crown South African Wine' every Christmas on UTV, the vapid voice-over hammering home the message that wine was to be drunk only once a year? Belfast restaurants – with a few honourable exceptions – offer lowest-common-denominator wines at top-whack prices, contributing to a disappointing experience overall for the discerning. Those that encourage you to 'bring your own' – and they are legion – are ill served by the dull chains of wine shops often located opposite them, where quality is rare and wine sales are more often determined by the odd shape of the bottles stocked than by any interest on the part of the owners in the fruit of the vine.

Happily, Ireland is improving all the time. The small producers, the wonderful markets, the brilliant chefs tirelessly pushing the country's restaurant food towards excellence are all ensuring that the future offers the prospect of a real food culture where not only will the food be excellent but the harmony of meals and foodstuffs will at last hold its own against the long-held traditions of the Latin countries.

We have always had brilliant produce – Continental chefs are green with envy on this score – but we used to butcher it. Jokes about 'yer mammy's vegetables', overcooked and devoid of nutritional value, have done the rounds for yours, but the know-how and respect shown to food has never been as great as it is now.

As Ireland has ascended in the food stakes, it is notable how much France, that former bastion of good eating, has deteriorated, a slide begun in the eighties. When I lived in France even school meals where brilliant: a five-course meal in the local *routier* cost €2 and was stunning in terms of both value and quality. Naturally, times have moved on pricewise, but it is difficult to accept that the country which influenced me so much in so many ways has in effect flown the coop gastronomically.

Meals in France are more often bad than good, supermarkets – once great – are now just all right, and the produce on offer at weekly village and town markets, while still superb in many ways, has nonetheless caught the bug too, and a marked deterioration is visible. Vegetables are often tired, salads flaccid, fish not quite as fresh as it might be – and worst of all, the French are accepting this situation.

Contrast this with street markets such as those in Galway and Dublin's Temple Bar and you can see what I mean. Already, these are markets dedicated to quality, to organic produce, to dazzling variety – and to fun. Sitting in the Temple Bar food fair scarfing half a dozen oysters with a couple of glasses of Muscadet only serves to underline how things have come almost full circle and makes me long for the France of just twenty-five years ago.

But then, I have it here now. It's great to be taking part in the food-orientated Ireland of today. Let's hope we realise what we have and nurture and cherish it. Slow-roast lamb with Thai sweet chilli crisps, anyone? Anyone?

This is a very simple dish to cook and uses everyday ingredients. The sauce and lentils add a sophisticated twist, though, and the result is very moreish. It's the sort of thing I like to cook quickly for myself or for the unexpected guests that I fantasise might pop by sometime (but never do). I haven't used cheese, but you could grate some Parmesan and sprinkle that over to finish.

4 chicken breasts
50g Puy lentils
2 red peppers
250g tagliatelle (or other pasta)
Glass of white wine
Salt and pepper
200ml cream
Butter

Serves 4

for the lentils:
Soak the lentils in water for about an hour. Drain and add to boiling water. Boil rapidly for about thirty minutes, but taste regularly, as they need to be al dente.

for the chicken:
Slice the chicken into medallions and grill or fry until cooked. Keep warm in an oven on a low heat.

for the red pepper:
Deseed the pepper, stripping away the white part, and cut it into thick slices. Place the slices of pepper skin-side up under a hot grill to blacken them. Once the sliced pepper has cooled slightly, peel away the black bits.

for the cream:
Into the pan you cooked the chicken (if you fried it), add a glass

of white wine and simmer to reduce. (This retains the delicious juices from the chicken.) Add the cream and seasoning to the wine and continue to simmer for a couple of minutes. Add a knob of butter and reduce on a medium heat for around five minutes.

for the pasta:
Put the pasta in a large saucepan of boiling salted water and simmer, as per cooking instructions. (Tagliatelle is ideal, but if you can find *pappardelle,* those mouth-satisying, even wider ribbon noodles, try using them. They look great on the plate and you can play with your presentation.) When the pasta is cooked, drain it and add ground black pepper, a pinch of salt and a knob of butter, then stir everything together until the butter has melted.

to serve:
Bring all the ingredients together and toss to coat in the cream. Alternatively, you could sauce the plates individually first, mix the pasta with the lentils, and then, using a large two-pronged fork, spear and arrange a large twist of pasta in the middle of the plate. Place the chicken and red pepper on top of and around the pasta.

I have never cared much for penne or its variants (such as the smaller *pennette)* – and probably even less for broccoli. But I will never forget eating this dish for the first time – in that temple of modern Italian cooking, the River Café in London – and wolfing it down. What genius came up with the idea marrying these two ingredients and transcending their native ordinariness?

Since first enjoying the softness of *pennette* against the crunch of broccoli, I have discovered a similar pasta which I adore called *garganelli.* This pasta was originally produced under the Fini brand, who also make one of the leading types of balsamic vinegar that we are so familiar with in Ireland. It is a source of endless fascination to me that a pasta which looks for all the world like penne can have such a different texture in the mouth and arouse such marvellous passions. There is a 'flap' folded over in the middle of each tube; I think it is this ridge which lifts the *garganelli* far beyond the mundanity of penne.

I am pleased to report that *garganelli* finally seems to be available at most leading supermarkets. If you find it, I would suggest using it rather than *pennette* in the following recipe. This is my take on the River Café's dish – a simple supper dish or starter that is a doddle to make and a pleasure to eat!

250g broccoli
Pinch of salt
400g *pennette* (or *garganelli* if available)
Chilli oil
Dried chilli flakes (also known as 'cracked harissa')
1 clove garlic, peeled and crushed
Small handful of pine kernels

Cook the broccoli florets in lightly salted water until they are just underdone. Drain immediately, refresh in cold running water and leave to one side. Cook the pasta in a large quantity of salted water until almost – but not quite – al dente.

Heat the chilli oil until it begins to smoke. Add the chilli flakes and garlic, remove the pan from the heat and swirl the chilli and garlic around in the pan. Finally, remove both the ingredients with a slotted spoon. Add the broccoli and pine kernels to the oil and warm through over a low heat.

Drain the pasta and add to the pan containing the broccoli and oil, with a little of the water the pasta was cooked in. Stir thoroughly together, then add the chilli-and-garlic mix back to the pan. Serve either in a large platter for several people, or individually in heated dishes.

This is one of the many pasta dishes which are usually not eaten with Parmesan cheese (see also *spaghettini alle vongole* on page 207).

DERRY

Poor old Derry. When I was a nipper, us Belfast wans heaped fierce scorn on the place. For us, it was a grey, uninteresting town that you passed through on your way to Donegal, the locals were much too serious, and they added 'hey' to the end of every sentence. (How we laughed when they actually elected a mayor called Mayor Haigh, hey.) Generally, it wasn't a place you could be bothered with until the Undertones put Derry parka chic on the map. All we had by way of competition was Stiff Little Fingers and Van Morrison, and sure that'd put the fear of God in anybody.

In those days you wouldn't go to Derry for a feed, and unfortunately that still wouldn't occur to you by and large, but the town that some love so well has changed massively for the better and is a place of great craic, laughter and good times. I say 'unfortunately' because Derry is not just a place for 'pints, song and sandwiches' and has many hidden culinary charms.

For many years, the Beech Hill Country House Hotel eight kilometres outside the city has been a paragon of luxury, with a glorious reputation for fine food. This is an astonishingly grand place, the welcome is genuine, the hospitality superb. Fans of the Ulster fry will here find one of the finest examples of it: not for nothing has the hotel won the 'Galtee Irish Breakfast Award'. Their Ardmore restaurant, under chef Niall Gorham, is reputed throughout the district and is today catering for the new 'leisure tourist' that Derry is enjoying: those thirty-five-pluses who seek a stress-free environment, sheer perfection, and the sourcing of local ingredients where possible. The Beech Hill has all this and more. (You will notice too on their website, *www.beech-hill.com*, that the house once belonged to the Ó Catháin clan. I must point out that I have no interest to declare here – except my indignation on behalf of my alleged murderous ancestors.) It was here that I first came to know the talents of one Noel McMeel, savouring his delicious and impressively presented food in the most elegant of surroundings. Noel is now in Castle Leslie, which is covered in the

34

chapter on Monaghan.

Derry's other great restaurant is of course the magnificent Browne's Bar and Brasserie on Bond's Hill, in the Waterside area of the city across the river. Finding such an establishment in what the Undertones once famously described as 'humpy Derry' is a delightful surprise – a little slice of modern Europe on the banks of the Foyle. Menus change frequently and, just like the Beech Hill restaurant, produce used is both organic and local where possible.

It comes as no surprise to learn that Browne's began life as a burger bar in 1985 but has since evolved into the fine establishment that it is today. In 1995, the owners, brother and sister Ivan and Elma Taylor, grasped the chance to buy the run-down bar and, along with head chef Frank Kivlehan, set out to change the concept radically and take a more creative approach. The daring menus certainly reflect this desire to create and innovate, but one eye is ever on twenty-first-century Ireland, such as with this item, which would make any Irishman salivate: Irish goat's cheese baked in spring onions, parsley and cayenne, served with hot soda bread.

Like all cities of its type, Derry has its fair share of Indian and Chinese restaurants on the banks of the Foyle, and chance visits to some of them – the Mandarin Palace on Queen's Quay and the India House on Carlisle Road – proved very worthwhile indeed. The India House especially could hold its own with many of the superb Indian restaurants to be found in Britain.

Walk on down the street from the Mandarin Palace and there is a little gem of a place at the back of the Guildhall called the Exchange on Queen's Quay. Under the direction of head chef Colin Harrigan, this place has become a better-than-average modern brasserie, lively and fun, its finger firmly on the pulse of modern international cooking, but with more than a nod to good old Irish food. It scores highly not just for the flair of its cooking but also for the lack of sting in its prices.

Derry locals, while extolling the virtues of a pint and a sandwich, are visibly and audibly proud that their city is finally gaining a reputation for good food. They will quickly inform you of that 'new Italian down by the riverside', and this or that other place. And all were of one voice where the Bistro in the Tower Hotel was concerned – so much so that this writer will simply have to take a wee jaunt up there soon and try it.

When walking the streets of Derry, there is a great sense of a laid-back attitude to life: locals are friendly and always seem to have time for the inquisitive stranger. One is struck too by the omnipresence of the Irish language. The Great James Street area seems to be almost a mini-Gaeltacht in itself, such is the amount of Irish-language-related activity: the sight of trendy young execs speaking in Irish into their mobile phones in the streets is a surprising but welcome one. Even the present incumbent in Derry's Mansion House is Irish-speaking.

Add to that a bookshop, a club and two cafés, one of which, An Bacús, is very deserving of a visit. In An Bacús, business is done through Irish should you wish, the food, service and coffee are all exemplary, and, for those who are interested, regular learners' classes are held over great coffee and freshly baked scones. It is an absolutely delightful place.

Just up the road, in Waterloo Street, there is a lesser 'Gaeltacht' area known as the Donegal or Gaoth Dobhair quarter. This area is composed essentially of bars that all have a Donegal theme. Try Peadar O'Donnell's or the Gweedore. Although a door connects the two of them, the music policy in each of them is quite different: the former specialises in traditional Irish music, whereas the latter has blues and rock bands.

For pub grub of a certain stamp, try Badgers next to the Millennium Forum, or the Delacroix on the Buncrana Road. It is here that you might encounter that Derry speciality 'poundies', which is what we Belfast wans call 'champ'. No doubt the Derrymen would claim some subtle differences in their mix, but as I said earlier, they're much too serious. Besides, which appellation has now spread to menus all over Ireland: champ or poundies?

Go on out of that!

They say Greek food always tastes better outside the country. Certainly my memories of food in Greece aren't too hot: mainly spag bol – though that may have had more to do with the state of the wallet of my eighteen-year-old self than anything fundamentally wrong with the nation's cuisine. Still, it was many years before I was introduced to the joys of Greek amd Cypriot cooking and the magic of feta cheese, *halloumi* (ewe's-milk cheese from Cyprus), olives, *dolmades* (stuffed vine leaves), *yemista* (stuffed vegetables), the delightful *spankopitta* (filo pastry with spinach, raisins and pine nuts), lamb's tongues and the often unfortunate moussaka (which is frequently as poorly executed outside its home country as lasagne). I have always enjoyed these delights, it has to be said, in Ireland or somewhere else that isn't Greece, however. The mystery of the state of food in the mother country must remain that way, as I have returned there.

Still, it was in the company of a Derryman, Dermot Doherty, now resident in Inis Eoghain, that I discovered the subject of this recipe: *kleftico*. I have since enjoyed it in many fine restaurants, but none of these servings has had such an effect on me as that first one in London at Christmas 1974. On that occasion, a marvellous, aromatic dish of divine lamb with mysterious new, satisfying and earthy flavours was served by Dermot's Cypriot brother-in-law.

A couple of years ago, I decided to put the dish on the menu in the restaurant in Belfast that I was working in. It was a huge hit: we couldn't make enough of it to satisfy the demand. And for us hard-worked chefs, it was a godsend: a slow-cooked triumph of lamb which, by its very nature, was prepared in advance, couldn't be ordered rare, medium or burnt, and never got overcooked – if you kept an eye on it. We partnered it with trendy crushed potatoes, a black-olive tapenade – which I felt to be very Mediterranean altogether – and a side salad of lettuce, tomatoes and grilled *halloumi* cheese.

The dish got its name from the word '*kleftis*', which means 'robber'. They say that, in the past, mountain men would cook their stolen meat in sealed, underground ovens. I recently visited

Cyprus and ate *kleftico* as it should be eaten: up a mountain, and straight from a clay-sealed oven. There seem to be many variants of the recipe; my version is hardly authentic and was tailored to suit local tastes, so don't be too hard on me if you know better.

The lamb of course is king. I used to get the butcher to cut me big lumps of rump or chump of lamb but you could also get a leg of lamb and ask him to cut it into eight pieces. Other recipes use broad chops (called 'gigot chops' in the Republic) or shanks: there is no reason why these cuts should not be used, because, as *kleftico* is a slow-cooked dish, the meat will be falling apart at the end – which is the desired effect. Herbs and garlic are de rigueur too.

Chunks of lamb (cut up by your butcher: shanks, rump, chump chops, broad (gigot) chops, or leg, cut into eight)
16 new potatoes, boiled
Olive oil
Half a bottle of red wine
1 lemon
1 onion, roughly chopped
Bay leaves
Mint, chopped
Tomatoes
6 cloves of garlic
Thyme
Rosemary
Coriander seeds
Pepper
Sea salt (Guerande)
Black olives
Halloumi cheese
2 CDs of *rembetika* music (the Greek blues)

Take your cut of meat, make incisions in it with a sharp knife and insert slivers of garlic. Place the meat in an oven dish that is big enough to accommodate your meat and deep enough to allow the meat to simmer in its own juices. Assuming that you've now got eight hefty pieces of lamb, liberally douse it with good olive oil, a glass (or two) of red wine (though white will do), a little lemon

38

juice, some finely grated lemon peel, a roughly chopped onion, some bay leaves, a handful of chopped mint, and several crushed garlic cloves. Then, like Monica and Richard in *Friends,* crush three or four tomatoes erotically over the mix with the palm of your hand. Some thyme, a little rosemary, a sprinkling of coarse sea salt and a scattering of coriander seeds completes the marinade, which smells wonderful. Leave it covered with aluminium foil for about three hours, or overnight if you can, to allow the aromatics to work on the meat.

When you're ready to cook the marinated lamb, make sure the oven is preheated to 180°C; place the dish in the oven – keeping the foil on top – and leave to bake for an hour and a half to two hours. You could simply serve it with crushed potatoes – young potatoes, literally crushed with a wooden spoon – and a little olive oil and salt and pepper to taste. I also add finely chopped black olives and cut an aubergine lengthways into medium-thick slices, soak each slice in olive oil and quickly grill the slices on both sides: just succulent. If you prefer, you could do the salad that I mentioned: toss some green leaves in olive oil and lemon juice (three parts oil to one part lemon juice), add tomatoes, olives if you fancy, and some grilled slices of *halloumi* cheese. *Halloumi* is completely uninteresting when raw but is exquisite, salty – and a perfect foil to the *kleftico* – when grilled.

Whatever accompaniments you decide to go for, serve to friends, open a few bottles of hearty red wine, turn the bouzoukis up and enjoy!

I admit that I was obsessed with food all my life, as far back as I can remember. And I'm sure that I made my first efforts to cook something at the age of six. Why fate then decided to place me in Belfast is anybody's guess.

My earliest gastronomic memories are of eating what we used to call 'willicks' (whelks or periwinkles) from a paper bag bought in a fishmongers on the Shankill Road. You ate them with a tiny pin, donated free of charge. The Shankill Road in the sunny pre-1969 days was a treasure trove of LPs and 45s too expensive for a twelve-year-old, American DC and Marvel comics to stare at, bric-a-brac, and these odd-looking but scrumptious willicks. It still seems very odd to me that a population that was then so loathe to try foreign foods, and so unloving of fish (except of course 'brown' fish on a Friday for almost half the population), should take to these strange sea snails so readily, and happily eat away at them while window-shopping.

But then the Troubles came, and I, a young Catholic, ceased to roam the Shankill as I had done in those carefree days. Not only that, but it seemed that a change of fashion had arrived, and the willicks of my childhood had all but disappeared – until 2001, when I revisited the Shankill Road for the first time in more than thirty years for episode one of my TV series for TG4, *Bia's Bóthar*. (Despite my cameraman's best attempts to expose me – and himself – as a Fenian by repeatedly screaming 'Do that walkie again, Éamonn!' at the top of his Free State voice, nobody batted an eyelid – a tribute to the brighter, better Belfast of today.) There we discovered Walter Ewing's excellent and long-established fishmongers, now a major supplier to Belfast's top restaurants, and feasted on his sublime smoked salmon outside 'on the Shankill', just like in the old days (though possibly a bit more upmarket). We then proceeded to the newly revamped St Georges Market in the centre of Belfast, where willicks are still on sale in paper bags among the freshest of fish, myriad olives and the old favourite, potato bread, or 'tattie bread', as it is known locally. You still get a free pin to eat the willicks with.

The other great traditional foodstuff was an edible seaweed called 'dulse', pronounced by Belfast people as *'dull-iss'*, indicating its derivation from the Irish *'duileasg'*. This is probably an even more curious treat than willicks, as it has a not-for-the-fainthearted flavour of the sea: that of salt and pure goodness. And yet generations chomped absent-mindedly on it. I can still remember being in my granny's house, where it seemed the whole family was sharing a bag in front of the telly, probably delighting in the 'can't tell margarine from butter' ads from Reddifusion in London. (By the by, the Stork test never came to Belfast: I assume their researchers knew that you couldn't fool Irish people where butter was concerned.)

Dulse is still sold all over Belfast, notably in fine-food shops such as that great institution Sawers, in the centre of town on Fountain Street. One no longer sees the family sharing a bag of the stuff, but, when in season, it is cheap and plentiful – and a fraction of the cost it fetches for fancy tables in Dublin. It struck me as odd, some years ago, that these days, when people will happily dine out on nori rolls, suck up samphire, and get all gooey over carrigeen moss, the humble Belfast delicacy dulse had never been incorporated into mainstream dishes by some clever-clever local chef. I successfully created some such dishes which I felt worked – but then I could never get a second opinion because nobody wanted to know. Raw dulse from a paper bag was one thing, but in dishes? In restaurants? With chilled vodka, for goodness sake? Notwithstanding this indifference, my simple recipe for *spaghettini* with dulse and smoked salmon is given below.

But then none of us growing up in the 1960s – even those six-year-olds uniquely obsessed with food, lost in a world of pavlova and Black Forest gateau – could have imagined today's Belfast, resplendent in its many restaurants. If the city is still not the leading light of gastronomy in Ireland, the years since the mid-1990s ceasefire have seen an explosion of another type, that of restaurants at every corner, displacing the corner pub – well, a wee bit anyway – and offering a dazzling array of foods, both native and foreign, which were unthinkable just a dozen years ago. Although Belfast is still debatably five years behind Dublin, it is certainly trying, and trying hard.

Belfast people love 'packing', and those foods which supply that – the ubiquitous Ulster fry and the fish supper – are still around and as popular as ever. The only real difference between today and the sixties is that you can now get an Ulster fry all day long. Other traditional foods are still prominent in Belfast and make for a hearty and inexpensive meal. In addition to the afore-mentioned Ulster fry, one can find the delightful champ almost everywhere. In fact, such is its popularity that it is now a staple on tables in Dublin and Cork. The secret of course is: don't mess with it. Smoked-chipotle champ is all very well, but it ain't champ: that appellation is reserved for the ultimate comfort food, which is mashed potatoes, milk, scallions and glorious butter. Irish stew too is ubiquitous. (Recipes for this dish vary from fam-ily to family, but the version sold in most establishments is the same as that enjoyed elsewhere in Ireland: lamb, potatoes, carrots – and long simmering.) One should not fail to try either of these wonderful dishes in places such as the listed Crown Bar, opposite the Europa Hotel (holder of the undesirable title of the world's most bombed hotel: thirty-four times, at last count) in Great Victoria Street or the Kitchen Bar in Victoria Square (shortly to relocate). And while a pint of plain may well be your only man, do try and seek out bottled Guinnes, long considered the superior form of the drink by Belfast connoisseurs, who never drank it chilled, the better to appreciate its nutty flavour.

When I was growing up in Belfast, more than a dozen bottlers had the right to issue labels on their Guinness – all with varying success (as the inferior brews could be readily identified) – but none was more famous, or more desirable, than Morton's 'Red Heart' Guinness. This was allegedly the brand that was forced upon patients per diem in hospitals in Belfast (or so we told each other). The unique Morton's label was to be found cheek-by-jowl with 'ordinary' Guinness on pub shelves. To get the former, you had to know the local parlance: thus a pint of Guinness was 'a pint of double' (as opposed to the now-defunct 'single X'), a bottle of Guinness was 'a bottle of stout', and a bottle of Red Heart was, well, 'a bottle of Red Heart'. It's still available in a few enlightened outlets: try the Morning Star in Pottinger's Entry off High Street for not only Red Heart but also great pub food. Fashion has determined that the great Belfast habit of drinking bottled Guinness has been superseded by the great Belfast habit of drinking pints of far-too-old Guinness, a fashion imposed by the brewing giant itself, though the good taste of Guinness drinkers would appear to be demanding the return of the pint at its classic temperature. In any case, ice-cold Guinness is better than Breó!

Those of us who were around at the start of the 1980s will remember the beginning of the end of the dark, food-free years when an enterprising Frenchman called Jean-Marie Delbart launched his first restaurant in Belfast, in dreary, dank Donegall Pass. Au Roi Jean was the first modern restaurant in Belfast: those of us who dined there will share a collective memory of great craic, of the veritable glow about the place, and especially of eating on the stairs, such was the demand for Delbert's food after years of gastronomic deprivation. We will also remember and salute the unknown wags who within forty-eight hours of the opening of the restaurant added a new graffito to its gable: 'Frogs Out.'

From there, we fast-forward to 1989 and the return of a Belfastman to his native town in search of premises – which he found in the shape of a disastrous establishment called Arabian Nights on Belfast's Shaftesbury Square. It was here that Roscoff was born. For many years, in this writer's opinion, Paul Rankin and his cooking made it the best restaurant in Ireland, and synonymous with excellent dining. Such was its excellence, and the keenness of its prices, that for once the advice *'vaut le détour'* ('worth making a detour for') was well-merited. Many's the time I travelled to Belfast by *Enterprise* from Dublin just to lunch or dine there – and afterwards I had change from what I would have spent on an equivalent meal in Dublin.

Today, Roscoff is no more, replaced by the snappier but no less excellent Cayenne, the jewel of Paul Rankin's empire, which now comprises cafés all over Belfast and a fun eatery, Rain City. Around the city centre, new and ever more exciting venues have sprung up. Yes, pizzerias and faux-Italian premises abound – Belfast loves cheap 'n' cheerful – but brighter and more daring restaurants now shine on the city's gourmet landscape.

43

Two thousand and three saw the establishment of Belfast's first city-centre Japanese restaurant, Zen, an awesome and expensive venture with chefs flown in from Tokyo to feed a local population baying for *osashimi* (raw fish), sushi (vinegared fish with rice) and tempura: the latter done properly at long last. And Michael Deane, already proprietor of both the award-winning Deane's Brasserie and the Michelin-starred Restaurant Michael Deane, added yet another success to his burgeoning empire with the opening of Chokdee on Bedford Street near the BBC. For a time, Tony O'Neill, who has worked extensively in Australia, perfecting his knowledge of pan-Asian food, was head chef there. Tony was responsible for some of the most memorable meals and Asian banquets ever enjoyed in the city in 2003 and 2004. Now back where he came from, in the snug little restaurant near Queen's University known as Beatrice Kennedy – a wonderful spot for Sunday lunch – he continues to cook some of the most exciting food in the city. One of his most memorable dishes from Chokdee – now on the menu in Beatrice Kennedy's – is his spicy crab-and-mango salad, a revelation of accurate and intuitive cooking. Tony has kindly supplied the recipe for this brilliantly simple dish below.

Finally, the restaurant to watch must be James Street South, found just behind Deane's, in the street from which it takes its name. It's oh-so-London, and very bright and clean, but nonetheless a welcome addition to the city, with superb cooking and very keen prices. Mention of prices prompts me to say that they serve Louis Roederer brut champagne at just £32 sterling a bottle, or a wallet-tempting £5.95 a glass. Compare that with   75, at best, in Dublin establishments. At that price, I frequently call in for a glass, just to cheer me up.

Of course, it's not just the centre of Belfast – known as 'downtown', and to be said in a sing-song accent – that has seen the growth of the restaurant industry. The suburbs too have witnessed the rise of the neighbourhood restaurant, in keeping with the drink-driving laws and the desire to dine out with a frequency that would have been unthinkable in my parents' day. A fine example of this development is to be found in my own local haunt, H20 in Dunmurry, a restaurant that would not be out of place in the city centre.

H2O, fronted by Marty and with Raymond in the kitchen, has been one of the locale's saving graces since the restaurant opened some eighteen months ago. The decor would not be to everyone's taste (being a bit 'eighties', as many reviewers have commented), and they really ought to do something about the music (which is often twee and intrusive), but the food, which is where it counts, is good. The menu veers towards the solidly traditional, even predictable, to entice plenty of bums onto seats, but also includes some much wittier dishes for the adventurous. Their squid is consistently excellent (would that it were always thus in other establishments), while my personal favourite – for which I return time and time again – has to be the Lebanese chicken, a spicy, satisfying supreme of chicken, perfectly cooked every time, with a counterpoint of *farika* – a sort of Lebanese couscous, cooked in rose-water, imparting a mouth-watering, subtle flavour. It comes with some grilled fennel and other accoutrements, and thoroughly deserves its title of Belfast's Best Suburban Dish – as long as you bear in mind that I just made that particular award up.

Add to this, attentive and concerned service, a good wine list, featuring many bargains, different menus for your different moods (such as a snack menu waiting in the wings should you not feel like the full three courses), different menus again for your *bambini*, great espresso, and that front-of-house man who gives up his Christmas Day just to open for you, and this is a restaurant that will give a great deal of pleasure.

Of course, when mentioning the rise of the suburban restaurant or the new foodie trails such as those of the Ormeau, Stranmillis or Dublin Roads, we cannot ignore the Lisburn Road, grandmammy of them all, where the ladies lunch at will in between the shoe shops and which is now awash with an incredible mix of cafés, casual restaurants, long-established Indian outlets, fine delicatessens, bread shops and the like. In fact, at the time of writing, I have just had several glasses of the most excellent wine, as well as a superb tapas meal in the Taps, the latest addition to Belfast's ever-changing restaurant scene. This establishment, on the Lisburn Road, has the most boozy, convivial atmosphere I have yet seen in Belfast: the dainty tapas, prepared by a lady chef from Barcelona, are both dazzling and delicious, the wine is heady, and friends are made at the drop of a menu.

Not so many years ago, I was laughed out of a city-centre delicatessen when I asked for peanut oil and spirit vinegar – basic ingredients for making a simple vinaigrette at home. I declined their well-intentioned offer of vegetable oil and malt vinegar. These days I can get just about anything I fancy, with the emphasis very much on variety and excellence. Belfast is on its way to becoming a gourmet's paradise, and long many it continue.

*

Further afield, other parts of County Antrim smack of wasted opportunity. When you consider that the north of the county is home to one of the world's great wonders, the Giant's Causeway, it is sad that many of the surrounding establishments are not yet up to par. Indeed, many of the local restaurants appear to be stuck in a time warp: the incredulity with which some humdrum requests are met is staggering. Recently I was served a full mug of espresso in a café in neighbouring Portrush when I asked for a single shot of the brew. The waitress simply could not comprehend that anyone could wish for anything less than a very large cup of coffee.

All is not lost, though. Try the Ramore Wine Bar at the harbour in Portrush for an unbeatable atmosphere and some terrific cooking from George McAlpine and his team. Further inland is the quaint village of Portballintrae – and Sweeney's Wine Bar, which also serves food. If you go into the village itself, a turn to the right will bring you down to the village of Bushmills, home of one of the greatest Irish whiskeys.

Bushmills itself is a fairly nondescript place. The distillery should of course be visited: it will while away an afternoon admirably. I have always been a fan of this fine whiskey, which is distilled three times – unlike its Scottish sibling, which is distilled twice. The smoky, peaty flavour is just so: smooth on the tongue and equally soft on your insides on the way down. If the classic 'Old Bushmills' is all this, then its sister whiskey, Black Bush, is all that and more. I adore Black Bush: for me, it is the king of

46

whiskeys, sheer perfection in a glass – a restrained and subtle blend of peat, smoke and barley. Not for me the upstart newcomer, Bushmills Malt. Leave it to the Scots to do that sort of thing, I say. (In their process, the malted barley is dried over peat fires, which accounts for the notes smoky taste of Scotch. In the making of Irish whiskey, the barley is dried in closed ovens and never comes into contact with smoke, leaving the malted-barley flavour to shine through.)

Across the road from the distillery is a house that offers no indication that anything lies within than some anonyomous inhabitants. Round the back you will find the entrance to the Bushmills Inn, a haven of fine cooking in north Antrim. It was here that UTV's Gerry Kelly hosted his live televised Paddy's Day bash link-up with New York a few years back. Inside is cosy, all nooks and crannies offering great lunches and dinners, plus an extremely well-stocked bar, with rare cognacs and other digestifs – if you dare drink anything other than Black Bush in its own home.

The county of Antrim sports many gourmet black spots, however. As its flawed tourist infrastructure takes stock of the new demands being placed on it by visitors, it will take a long time for it to catch up with the rest of the country. But as surely as the country takes its manners from the city, and rarely the other way around, the influence of Belfast and its dashing new restaurant culture will be felt on its own county before too long.

SPAGHETTINI WITH WALTER EWING'S
SMOKED SALMON AND DULSE

This is a very simple dish to make, but some care should be taken with both the dulse and the salt. Chop the dulse as finely as possible and use sparingly: the idea is just to fleck the pasta with it and give a hint of the flavour of the sea. Since the dulse will have its own salty flavour, salt should be used only in the water in which the pasta is cooked. If you think that the dish may not be salty enough, place sea-salt crystals on the table and let your guests add their own.

> 1 packet of quality *spaghettini*
> 1 slice per person of Walter Ewing's smoked salmon
> 1 tub crème fraiche
> 1 bag dulse
> 1 bunch chives
> Naggin of.vodka
> Cracked black pepper
> Sea salt

Serves 4

Place the bottle of vodka in the freezer well in advance; it will not burst. Boil a pot of water with a decent pinch of sea salt added. When the water boils, add the *spaghettini,* which should take only a few minutes to cook. Finely chop the chives, reserving a few sprigs for the garnish; chop the dulse. Fashion the smoked salmon slices into rosettes and put to one side.

When the *spaghettini* is cooked al dente, drain and return it to a wide frying pan with a little of the cooking water. Stir in the chopped dulse, followed by the crème fraiche, the chives and a little cracked black pepper to taste. Thoroughly coat the pasta with the crème-fraiche mixture, which will be warmed through by the pasta.

Insert a large, two-pronged carving fork into the middle of the pasta and roll the pasta into a ball; transfer it to a hot plate. Arrange the rosette of salmon on top. Open the bottle of vodka, place your thumb over the top and pour a slug of the spirit over the salmon. Arrange a few chive leaves attractively on top – and that's it. Oh, and you could serve the dish with a schooner of the chilled vodka to drink!

for the salad:
250g white crab meat
2 baby gem lettuce, leaves removed and torn in half
1 ripe mango, peeled and sliced
14 fresh mint leaves
12 coriander leaves
4 scallions, finely sliced
2 red shallots, finely sliced
8 cherry tomatoes, cut in half
1 small cucumber, peeled, deseeded and sliced

for the dressing:
500ml vegetable oil
2 shallots, finely diced
1 tablespoon red curry paste
1 large knob of ginger, peeled and diced
4 red chillies, deseeded and chopped
100g palm sugar, grated
100ml rice wine vinegar
Juice of 2 limes
50ml fish sauce
Coriander, chopped

Serves 4

To make the dressing, heat three tablespooons of the oil in a wok and add the shallots, curry paste, ginger and chillies. Fry over a medium heat and cook until the paste smells fragrant. Add the sugar and vinegar and cook until the ingredients form a light syrup. Remove from the heat and stir in the lime juice, the fish sauce and the remaining oil. Finally, add the coriander, and taste to make sure the flavours are well balanced. It should be hot, sweet, sour and salty, with no one taste overpowering the others.

To make the salad, place all the salad ingredients in a bowl and mix well. Add four to five tablespoons of the dressing and mix well. Arrange in a large bowl and serve. This salad works well on its own for a light lunch or is a strong start to a meal, but I find it is at its best if served in the Thai manner – in a banquet with several other Thai dishes and a big bowl of steamed jasmine rice.

ROAST LOIN OF ORGANIC PORK WITH A SAUCE OF BLACK BUSH WILD IRISH HONEY AND GREEN PEPPERCORNS

1 piece boned and rolled loin of pork
Glass dry white wine
1 tablespoon white-wine vinegar
200ml cream
Small glass Black Bush
Dollop of honey
Small jar of green peppercorns
Stock (optional)
Chilled butter, cubed
Salt and pepper

vegetables to accompany:
Potatoes (preferably Charlotte), par-boiled
Spinach
8 cherry tomatoes, slow-roasted

Serves 4

This is a very straightforward dish. The roast should first be browned all over: place it in an oven dish on the hob and fry in a small amount of butter. Then put it in the oven until cooked – thirty to forty minutes – leaving the meat just pink.

Remove the meat from the dish and leave to cool. It will then be easier to carve and will continue to cook in its own heat.

Return the dish to the top of the cooker, turn up the heat and deglaze with white wine and a splash of vinegar (to incorporate the flavours from the bits of roasted meat that remain on the pan). When this has reduced, strain into a saucepan, add the stock (if using), reduce, and then add a little cream. When thickened, stir in some diced, chilled butter. Finally, add the honey to taste, and a splash of Black Bush. The combination of the smoky whiskey, with its overtones of turf, contrasts very well with the subtle sweetness of the honey. The pungency of the green peppercorns balances the whole dish.

The cooked potatoes should be halved and grilled with herbes de Provence on a hand-held grill pan. Arrange the carved meat slices around a mound of buttered spinach, leaving it slightly exposed (to add colour to the dish). Sauce around this arrangement and place two slow-roasted cherry tomatoes in the sauce. Then place the grilled potato halves around the edge of the plate. Sprinkle two or three green peppercorns on the meat itself.

Apart from those served in the Dublin restaurants Vermilion and Poppadum, the Indian dish that has impressed me most in recent years has been Paul Rankin's shank of lamb *rogan josh*, which he served me in his flagship Belfast restaurant, Cayenne. Shank of lamb is of course dead trendy – and still dead cheap – and I think this cut suits the dish perfectly. (I do not purport to offer Paul's recipe here. This is mine; I've just nicked the idea from him.)

'Rogan josh' means 'red meat'. The colour comes from the addition of crushed red chillies, or paprika for a milder version. You may use lamb or beef. Serve with rice, either good basmati or Tesco's 'easy-cook'. (Always buy the opaque kind of rice, never the white.)

   6 to 8 cloves garlic
   1 teaspoon salt
   1-inch length of fresh root ginger, chopped
   6 to 8 tablespoons vegetable oil
   1kg (2lb) lamb shoulder or leg of stewing beef, cut into
       one-inch cubes
   2 bay leaves
   8 to 10 cardamoms (I use about 6 green and 4 black)
   6 cloves
   10 peppercorns
   Cinnamon stick
   2 large onions
   2 to 4 red chillies, deseeded and chopped
   1 tablespoon paprika
   One and a half teaspoons coriander seeds
   2 teaspoons cumin seeds
   6oz plain yoghurt

Crush the garlic with the flat of a blade and then add the salt to make a paste. Chop the ginger and add it to the garlic with a little water. Blend in a blender and add water until you have a thick paste. (This paste can be made in larger quantities and kept in a jar in the fridge for four to six weeks.)

In a wide pan, heat a little oil until it smokes, then sear the meat. Brown on all sides. Set aside.

Heat the cardamoms to split them and add them, with the cloves, bay leaves, cinnamon and peppercorns, to the oil for a few seconds until they swell. Add the garlic-ginger paste and stir for a few seconds, then add the sliced onions, turn the heat down and sweat for seven to ten minutes, deglazing the pan with the onion juices. Grind the coriander and cumin. (I use a coffee mill for this. You can use pre-ground spices, but I urge you to find whole spices: it makes all the difference.) Add the chillies and stir, add the ground spices and paprika and stir, put the meat and any juices back in the pan and stir.

Add the yoghurt a tablespoonful at a time, stirring to reduce. Add water (half a pint for lamb, three-quarters of a pint for beef). Bring to the boil, cover and put in an oven at 180°C for one hour for lamb, two hours for beef. Remove and stir occasionally. (You can cook this on a stove if you like: part-cover the pan and stir frequently.) About ten minutes before serving, remove the lid and reduce until you have a thick red sauce.

DOWN

County Down is an awful nuisance for a car-less individual like myself, and a county I have difficulty getting a handle on. It seems to be all over the place, going up (from where I live) to Bangor and also down – far down – to places like Newry and Newcastle. But then, since I was quite hopeless at geography as a spotty lad, obtaining an 'F' for fail, that should come as no surprise.

Apart from its girth, it also has a ruddy great peninsula in which Strangford Lough is ensconced, but which serves to make the county very, very pretty. Thinking of the beautiful lough and the countryside around it, I am here prompted to offer a 'tip for the lads'. Should you wish to make an impression on a young lady (especially one who isn't actually from County Down), take her on a drive to Strangford and get the five-minute ferry across to Portaferry, where, after dazzling her with the short crossing, you will take her for lunch. This brings us rather neatly to our first restaurant in County Down: the Narrows in Portaferry. Here is a warm welcome, great food and drink, simply splendid foie gras betimes and, when you're in luck, the sight of the light shining on the water outside with a glistening effervescence that is magical to behold. Except that, of course, gentleman that you are, you will have your back to it.

Of course, you could have taken her to the Cuan in Strangford before getting the ferry, or the snuggy Lobster Pot just across the street from the Cuan. These are just a few of the many splendid restaurants in County Down: if our new-found restaurant culture in Ireland has been a little slower in hitting the north of the country, County Down has taken to it more enthusiastically than the other northern counties combined.

It's not that far back that there were few good restaurants to speak of: my memory is of one long fish-and-chip trail from the seafront at Bangor to, well, the seafront at Newcastle. In the sixties and seventies (and still today), families thought nothing of eating hot and heavy fast food in what passed for sunshine (of course there was a lot more of it then), often consumed in a hot and stuffy car with the windows half rolled down, the smell of ghastly malt vinegar emanating forth. The only major changes in the fast-food arena since then have been the addition of kebabs and the omnipresent hamburgers and the unremarked loss of a dried-potato product called Chipples, eaten in hulking great sandwiches fashioned with a bread called Mother's Pride.

Fortunately, major changes have occurred in the restaurant scene: these days one is spoilt when visiting the county, for in addition to the many fine restaurants, there are also quite a few grand ones, with attendant Michelin stars. Again, not so long ago, Michelin stars were simply unheard of in Ireland, and particularly in Ulster. It wasn't until Paul Rankin earned the first one for Belfast with his flagship Roscoff restaurant that the floodgates opened: local chefs Michael Deane and Robbie Millar followed closely on his heels.

The original Deane's on the Square in its original situation within the old station building at the charming Helen's Bay was one of my favourite restaurants in the north. One of life's greatest pleasures had to be going there on the train from Belfast, cross-city, for Sunday lunch, alighting from the train and heading straight from platform to dining room, only to repeat the exercise in reverse after a scrumptious lunch, sauntering airily and somewhat refreshed to the up platform for the return train to Belfast. Sure, the waiter would even advise you of the approaching train, which arrived on the half-hour. The only decision was whether to miss it and get the next one after (oh, I might as well admit it) yet another Calvados. I'm sorry to have whetted your appetite, as now I have to tell you that the restaurant is no longer there. These days, Michael has relocated to Howard Street in the centre of Belfast – and taken his star with him. But I couldn't leave out the story of the restaurant in the railway station in County Down.

Shanks, which earned its Michelin star in 1996, is situated just outside Bangor at the Blackwood Golf Centre on the Clandeboye estate. Robbie was number two in Roscoff for many years before opening Shanks with his wife Shirley and quickly earning the coveted star. While dinner is naturally enough a terrific experience – I still have dreams about the smoked-chilli polenta I had there – my preference would be for lunch. An afternoon can be whiled away at Shanks looking out on the estate – from which some of the produce for the menus come – or marvelling at the ballet-like and effortless precision of the chefs visible through the windowed kitchen.

We'll come back to the stars presently, but especial mention must be made of the fact that this is the land of inns and hostelries, where visitor and local alike can pamper themselves with a special treat. Among the finest of these establishments are the Old Schoolhouse Inn in Comber and of course the Old Inn in Crawfordsburn, not far from Bangor. The latter is not only one of the most comfortable, luxurious and cosy places around for a drink but also boasts a superb restaurant with mouth-watering menus. I ate there recently with my young son in their Parlour Bar (there are three distinct food areas). I enjoyed an afternoon snack – an open prawn sandwich – that was promptly and perfectly served, and my little gastronome in shorts was also brilliantly catered for. His 'hot *panino* from the griddle' was, he declared, 'gorgeous'.

We cannot, will not, ignore the Buck's Head in Dundrum. Not only is the drive there from Belfast itself rather pleasant, but the view of the timeless Mourne Mountains as you approach the village of Dundrum is quite breathtaking. The Buck's Head itself is a lovely old pub with both traditional and more modern dining rooms, each of which offers the same contemporary menu. By contemporary, I mean a menu which not only incorporates influences from the modern school of cooking – Asian, European and Pacific Rim – but also is not afraid to deliver such stalwarts as champ, oysters and lamb. The cooking is stylish, with sensible portions, and there is always room for the unusual. Recently, following a great lunch, I had the most excellent dessert there, accompanied by espresso-soaked prunes which were simply exquisite. I have been known in my time to soak Agen prunes in tea (preferably Darjeeling, darlings) and rum (preferably Martiniquan, loves), but espresso? It never occurred to me. Suffice to say that the prunes were sublime, taking on a succulent, near-meaty timbre, with a length of flavour and impact that was almost hallucinogenic.

There is obviously no shortage of fine eating houses in County

Down then, but what good would they be without wine? Tucked away in the lovely village of Crossgar is Jim Nicholson's shop, home to possibly the finest selection of wines in Ireland. Jim has been twenty-five years in business and now supplies the leading establishments all over the country, with outlets in Crossgar and Dublin. Visiting the neat little shop, glittering with its gems of the vine, is a rare pleasure: there is nowhere quite like it. I suppose I'm prejudiced, since it offers some of my favourites from the Rhône Valley, such as M. Guigal's La Mouline, La Turque and La Landonne, still at quasi-sensible prices. The list seems endless: only the best from the world's greatest wine-producing areas are on offer, and many of the offerings are exclusive to Jim's shops.

These days, however, the real Star of the County Down is the restaurant Oriel, situated in Gilford. This eating place has been owned by Barry Smith for the past five years and has gone under the name 'Oriel' (after the ancient kingdom of Oirghialla, which straddled the area) since September 2000. It was awarded a Michelin star in January 2004. The village of Gilford is anything but picture-postcard pretty, and Oriel is an unassuming building tucked away at one end of the village, itself a ten-kilometre drive from Portadown. Indeed, when I meet the affable Barry, he seems almost apologetic for the decor of his restaurant, explaining that people are now coming from far and wide and that some of the more toffee-nosed elements are surprised, nay disappointed, with the homely nature of his starred establishment.

But it quickly becomes apparent that this chef-patron is an eater – that is, one who takes the trouble to taste and eat the food that he cooks as well as paying regular visits to rival establishments to check them out. Salivating while describing his admiration for Gordon Ramsey's London restaurant ('my favourite', he beams), he quietly explains how he put all his money and efforts into the food first and foremost, concentrating on getting that right, in the belief that the surroundings would receive attention as the restaurant went from strength to strength. I am delighted to hear this: the standard of the food in my own restaurant far outclassed that of the premises. For the record, I thought Barry's place looked great.

Barry describes his fare as 'modern Irish with strong French influences', and the menu reads as an absolute treat. Local ingredients are used wherever possible, while fresh vegetables and salads are delivered from the vast market at Rungis in Paris each week. He recalls how it wasn't easy at first to change from the established menu, which he inherited from the previous incumbent, the Yellow Door. Mindful of his patrons and the demands of the locale, menus were initially slow to change; when they did, the reaction was not overwhelmingly enthusiastic, and the owners often anguished over whether they had done the right thing. But their perseverance paid off as word got around: these days, Barry proudly recounts how Dubliners make the trip up just to eat there and will often stay the night in the local hotel. While the use of local ingredients is to be encouraged, it is a pleasure to see the extensive use of 'all-Ireland' ingredients such as Wicklow lamb crusted with cepes, while that firm favourite Clonakilty black pudding is partnered with a slow-braised belly of Ulster pork.

While the menus are typical of Michelin-starred establishments in that they offer both an à la carte and a tasting menu, the prices are anything but. The person who is prepared to undertake, in Michelin parlance, le détour will certainly not find himself short-changed.

There is one other fabulous surprise, and that is Oriel's Sunday-lunch menu. I was delighted to discover that such existed, and cannot wait to take myself down there by Enterprise to Portadown and then by taxi to Gilford in the very near future. The three-course meal costs just £21 sterling and includes such wonderful delights as samosas filled with lamb shank, the aforementioned Ulster pork belly (which I reckon is a must-eat), a daube of beef, and of course the ubiquitous champ – which here achieves the nirvana status that befits it. Reading the menu and talking about it to Barry, I was instantly reminded of my old Sunday-lunch trips to Deane's on the Square. Oh and there's also panna cotta for dessert. If only Oriel was in a railway station.

I was so taken with the menu on offer at Oriel that I begged Barry Smith for a couple of his recipes. Generous to a fault, he has kindly supplied me with the two that he saw caught my beady eye.

BRAISED BELLY OF ULSTER PORK, CREAMED SAVOY CABBAGE, SHALLOT PURÉE AND SHERRY-VINEGAR GLAZE

This cheaper cut of pork, which is currently on our winter menu, is packed with lovely rich caramelised flavours: real comfort food! I like to serve it with Clonakilty black pudding and a creamy roast-garlic-and-truffle *pomme purée*. When ordering the meat, insist on fresh local pork, and ask your butcher to remove the skin and bone for you.

    1kg pork-belly joint, skinned and boned
    50ml olive oil
    50g rosemary, chopped
    25g thyme, chopped
    6 cloves garlic
    1 small carrot, roughly chopped
    1 celery stick, roughly chopped
    1 small leek, roughly chopped
    1 onion, roughly chopped
    3 star anise
    2 teaspoons coriander seeds
    2 teaspoons black peppercorns
    50g rock salt
    1200ml brown stock (we use a chicken stock)
    150ml sherry vinegar
    200ml soy sauce
    100ml port

    for the creamed cabbage:
    1 small savoy cabbage
    25g unsalted butter
    200ml double cream

for the shallot purée:
400g shallots, peeled and finely sliced
50g unsalted butter
100ml double cream
10ml black-truffle oil (optional)

for the sherry-vinegar glaze:
1 shallot, finely sliced
50ml sherry vinegar
10g cubed butter, ice-cold

Serves 4

for the pork:
Lay the pork flat on a roasting tray and sprinkle with rock salt and freshly ground black pepper. Finely slice three cloves of garlic and press evenly into the pork flesh. Sprinkle the pork with the chopped rosemary and thyme and press well into the meat. Cover and place in the fridge for at least six hours.

Remove from the fridge and scrape the rosemary, thyme and garlic off with the back of a knife. Keep the rosemary and thyme. Roll the pork tightly into a pinwheel and tie firmly with string. Heat a heavy pan or iron casserole dish, lightly cover with olive oil, and brown the pork joint until it is well caramelised. Remove from the pan and add the carrot, celery, leek, onion and remaining garlic. Sauté until well coloured. Deglaze the pan with the sherry vinegar and reduce by half, then add the port and reduce by half again.

Tip the vegetables and pan juices into a suitable-size roasting tin or casserole, add the chicken stock, soy sauce, star anise, coriander seeds, black peppercorns, and the rosemary and thyme from the marinade. Cover with a lid of tin foil and braise slowly for four hours at 170°C, turning occasionally and basting in the cooking liquor. To test that it is done, push a metal skewer into the centre of the pork: it should be very soft and meltingly tender.

Remove the pork from the cooking liquor and set aside. When slightly cooled, cut the string from the pork and cut the meat into 6cm pieces. Sear on on all sides in a hot pan with some olive oil to give a nice golden colour. Strain the cooking liquor through muslin, skim off any fat, and set aside.

for the shallot purée:
Melt the butter in a pan, season, and sweat the sliced shallots for about eight to ten minutes, until they are soft and translucent. Then add the double cream, bring to the boil and simmer for three minutes. Blend in a liquidizer and pass through a fine sieve. Spoon into a clean saucepan and set aside.

for the sherry-vinegar glaze:
Sweat the shallots in a knob of butter for about eight minutes, until soft and translucent. Add the sherry vinegar and reduce by half, add the port and reduce by half, then add 600ml of the pork cooking liquor. Return to the boil and simmer until reduced to a shiny brown glaze. Finish the sauce by vigorously whisking in the ice-cold butter over a gentle heat.

to assemble the dish:
Heat four large bowls or plates, spread the shallot purée into an even circle in the centre, place a small round cutter on top and spoon in the creamed cabbage. Place the piece of pork on top of the cabbage and spoon the sauce around the outside. Serve with a rich, silky *pomme purée.*

20 fresh mussels
20 fresh cockles
250ml dry white wine
2 shallots, peeled and sliced
30g unsalted butter
6 large scallops, shucked and cleaned,
    with corals removed and halved
Pinch curry powder
30ml fish stock
1 shallot, finely diced
1 teaspoon root ginger, finely chopped
2 tbsp chives, finely chopped
250ml double cream
Half a cucumber, seeds removed, cut into 1cm dice
1 tablespoon coriander leaves, finely shredded
Sea salt (Maldon)

for the pasta:
230g plain flour
Pinch salt
2 eggs
3 egg yolks
1 tablespoon olive oil

Serves 4

for the pasta:
put the flour and salt in a food processor and add the eggs and oil. Blend until the mixture comes together. Tip onto a lightly floured surface and knead for five minutes until smooth. Wrap tightly in clingfilm and place in the refrigerator for one hour. Remove from the fridge and knead until smooth and pliable. Take a small piece of the dough, flatten it out and feed it through the thickest setting of a pasta machine, then reduce the setting and repeat until you

have reached the thinnest setting. Dry the pasta sheet slightly by hanging it over the back of a clean chair for ten minutes. Attach the noodle cutter to the pasta machine and carefully pass the pasta through, catching it on a lightly floured tray. Alternatively, buy some from your local supermarket!

for the cockles and mussels:
Wash the cockles and mussels thoroughly in cold water, discard any that are open or damaged and remove any beards. Heat a heavy-based saucepan until very hot, add the cockles, mussels, shallot, butter and white wine, and season with salt and freshly ground pepper. Cover with a lid and shake the pan occasionally. After three or four minutes the shells should all be opened. Strain, keeping the cooking liquor for the sauce. When cool, remove the cockles and mussels from their shells.

for the sauce:
Heat a knob of butter in a small saucepan, add the diced shallot and cook gently without colouring for ten minutes. Add the chopped ginger and 30ml of the mussel stock and reduce by half. Add the fish stock and reduce by half again. Pour in the cream, bring back to a gentle simmer and set aside.

to finish the dish:
Cook the linguini in a large pot of boiling salted water for one to two minutes, until it is al dente. Season the scallops with the sea salt and curry powder. Heat a non-stick pan and lightly coat with olive oil. Cook on each side for about forty seconds until just cooked. Finish the sauce by straining the cream into a clean saucepan. Bring back to a gentle simmer and add the cucumber, cockles, mussels, chives and coriander. To assemble the dish, swirl the pasta with a fork and place in the centre of a large bowl. Spoon the fricassée of cockles and mussels evenly around the pasta and place three pieces of seared scallop on top. In the Oriel, we would normally finish this dish with oyster tempura, or some fresh Oscietra caviar for really special occasions.

ARMAGH

The very first song I learned to sing was 'The Boys from the County Armagh'. It was a showpiece number that my parents encouraged me to sing sometime between the ages of three and five: I can still remember them beaming proudly as I caterwauled to the assembled company. Since then, of course, I have learned that I haven't a note in my head, and I have never again inflicted my ghastly voice on anyone. I suppose that Armagh was the first county that I ever heard of in 'my own Irish home'. For that reason alone, it has always had a special place in my head, even if I'm still not over-familiar with its terrain.

Armagh is known as the Orchard County – which appellation drew me to it – but the modern county is much more famous for its devotion to the GAA and the Irish language, its planetarium, its world-class pipers, its beautiful songs in the folk tradition (other than my own little music-hall number), and of course its cathedral city. Apart from the fruit-filled orchard heartland around Loughgall, various admirable attempts at food production have been tried and have been successful, at least for a while.

Most notable was the snail production during the 1990s, which, while laudable, was hardly guaranteed to last, given that Irish consumption was never likely to match that of the French. But for a time, proud of the fact that something as intrinsically foreign as the snail-raised-as-food was being produced in an Ulster county, I daringly put them on menus while cooking at Fitzers in the RDS in Dublin in the mid-1990s. These snail dishes were met with a mixture of curiosity, derision and excitement, and sold very well indeed – though unfortunately not enough to help support continued snail production in Armagh.

The other major development in the county was the introduction of wild boar some years back – the first time that a herd had been reintroduced into Ireland for four hundred years. For a time, many rare-breed cuts of County Armagh wild boar, as well as boar sausages and burgers, were seen on restaurant tables the length and breadth of the country. Again, as with the snails, boar

66

production has stalled and supply has ceased, until a sympathetic farmer can be found to take over the production once more. The boar were introduced by Gillian Dougan of Moyallon Foods – the company was established in 1991 to market the family's own farmed wild boar – and her fine company continues to be responsible for supplying the chefs and food shops of the region and beyond with an extensive range of local Irish and European foods. She always seeks out the traditional, the artisanal, those foods that have been farmed by free-range methods, and above all, those that are in season.

But, boys-a-dear, no one would claim County Armagh to be at the cutting edge of gastronomy in Ireland. Attempts have been made to open restaurants in many Armagh towns and villages but for the time being the county does not fare as well as neighbouring County Down. All is not gloom, though: the visitor should try the excellent Seagoe Hotel in Portadown or the legendary Famous Grouse in Loughgall, which specialises in local produce and offers both traditional and modern menus.

Like many of the chefs mentioned in this book, I have felt the influence of Thailand. Unlike so many of them, I have never been to Thailand to experience the food at first-hand or to pick up recipes. The closest I ever got was a restaurant in Orchard Road in Singapore, where my order was met with such incomprehension that I quickly gleaned that our 'three-course meal' method of eating in Thai restaurants at home in Ireland was a nonsense: I ended up with the table covered in food, which was impossible for me to do justice to – but which at least provided many chuckles for the bemused staff.

Here are a couple of recipes that I've been using for years. I have no idea where I got them from, just that they work and are simple to prepare. They give pleasure to my guests and make me feel rather pleased with myself when I execute them.

The roast pork used here could be replaced by other meats, including, for example, leftover turkey at Christmas.

Peanut oil
Small bowl of shallots, thinly sliced
Small bowl of garlic, thinly sliced
500g roast pork, thinly sliced
3 carrots, shredded
4 tomatoes, deseeded and julienned
5 scallions, cut into stips
Small bowl of red onion, thinly sliced
Small handful fresh mint, finely chopped
Small handful fresh coriander, finely chopped
Fresh lime juice
Nam pla (Thai fish sauce)
2 tablespoons sugar
Dried chilli flakes
Cos lettuce leaves, washed and dried
Cashew nuts, roasted and finely chopped

Pour oil to a depth of 25cm into a deep pan and heat. Add the shallots to the oil and cook until crisp. Remove these and drain them on kitchen roll. Cook the garlic in the same way.

In a large bowl, combine the pork, carrots, tomatoes, scallions, onion, mint and coriander. Whisk the lime juice, *nam pla,* sugar and chillies. Toss the leaves in this dressing.

Arrange the lettuce leaves on a serving plate and sprinkle with the cashew nuts. Finally, add the fried shallots and garlic and serve.

for the sauce:
3 cloves garlic
3 to 5 hot red chillies, deseeded and chopped
Bunch of chopped coriander
Fresh lime juice
1 tablespoon sugar
1 tablespoon *nam pla*
Salt

for the fish:
1 whole fresh fish such as sea bass, red snapper or even hake,
   gutted and cleaned.
2 stalks of fresh lemongrass
3 or 4 fresh kaffir lime leaves
3 slices fresh galangal

Crush the garlic, chillies, coriander and salt to a paste, preferably
using a mortar and pestle (otherwise in a blender). In a small bowl,
whisk together the lime juice, sugar and *nam pla*. Then add the
garlic paste and set the sauce to one side. Rinse the fish and then
dry it. Make four slits in the flesh and rub it all over with salt.
Stuff the cavity of the fish with the lemongrass, lime leaves and
galangal. Using a steamer or a wok with a plate ring, steam the fish
for fifteen minutes. Serve immediately. Pour a little of the sauce
over the top and serve the rest in a bowl. Serve with jasmine rice.

SNAILS WITH LINGUINI, APPLE CRISPS AND RICARD CREAM

Nothing arouses as much shouting, roaring and arm-waving among the world's English-speakers as the snail – and the eating of it. Most people express horror and claim that they would never indulge, yet I have found that any time I put them on the menu, in a variety of guises, Irish people were only too happy to order them. In fact, they often became one of the most popular starters on offer.

Maybe it was the way I did them? The classic approach is to cook them in their shells with snail butter (or *beurre mâitre d'hôtel*), an invigorating blend of butter, parsley and garlic. Snails like these were generally bought in a tin. For a short while there was some snail-farming in County Armagh, which was a very exciting development, and I had them on my menu permanently in Dublin in the wake of the 1995 ceasefires. With Armagh wild boar as a main course, I thought it a terribly good 'hands across the border' menu.

Since they were fresh, there was no need to serve them in their shells. A new approach was needed: I thought back to a dish I'd had at Simon Hopkinson's hand in London some years previously, and adapted it accordingly. However, what should have been a witty half-dozen snails on snail-buttered spinach inside a toasted brioche quickly became known among the diners of Dublin 4 as a 'snailburger', and the item was dropped.

I have no idea what made me think of flaming them in Ricard, but I did – and partnered them with linguini and a little cream sauce. It looked – and sold – well. But it could have been even better. Shortly afterwards, I had a dessert at Conrad Gallagher's first Peacock Alley which involved Ricard and apples, which had been flamed in same. Wonderful! If I'd only discovered this a little sooner, wouldn't Armagh apples have complemented the Armagh snails admirably?

Sadly, the Armagh snail is no longer with us. But here's the recipe: the twelve-inch-remix version. Just buy some tinned snails in any good delicatessen.

Half a packet of linguini
150ml cream
200ml chicken stock
Bunch of chervil
2 apples
6 snails per person
Shot of Ricard
Small glass of white wine
Butter
Salt and pepper.

First, slice the apples thinly and fry in a little butter until golden and crispy on each side. Pour a little Ricard into the pan and flame the apples, then remove and place on a heated plate.

Put the linguini on to cook in a pot of boiling salted water. Turn the heat up under the pan, add the chicken stock and reduce with a little white wine. When this has begun to thicken, add the cream and swirl around to form a sauce. Season and taste.

In a small pot, heat the rest of the wine and a sprig of chervil and add the snails to that, leaving to simmer for a minute or two. This is the best way to put a bit of life into the tinned variety of snails: fresh is, of course, best.

Heat some large pasta bowls. Drain the pasta and return to the pot with a little of the cooking water. Add finely chopped chervil, butter and plenty of black pepper. Roll a small amount of pasta per person onto a large fork and place in the centre of the bowl. Place a few apple slices on the plate and put the snails on and around those. Pour a little of the sauce around the apples. A sprig of chervil on top of the pasta, a final twist of the black pepper mill, and it's snail heaven!

MONAGHAN

There's no denying that it was Paul McCartney who put Castle Leslie on the international stage by choosing it for his recent marriage, though his former Beatle pal Ringo upstaged him in the who-is-still-looking-great stakes by looking so damn cool as he alighted at Aldergrove Airport on his way to the bash.

In Ireland we know better, of course, because Castle Leslie and Monaghan have long been on the Irish gastro-trail thanks to the efforts and talents of one man, Noel McMeel, head chef at this most 'mildly eccentric' of locations for some years now.

As stated elsewhere, I first came across Noel's food when he was chef at the Beech Hill outside Derry: I enjoyed memorable meals there on several occasions. Despite the luxurious nature of the setting, I was never distracted from the daring-but-simple food put in front me, whose poise and balance intrigued me. The dishes were pretty as a picture but also had that freshness that comes from having just left the chef's hand and being brought to the table in a twinkling.

Take his tagliatelle, for example. It was twisted into a hillock and still had steam rising off it, a helter-skelter of cascading strands of perfectly cooked fine pasta. Each and every length of pasta came apart as though the mound had been interweaved by hand in the first place, each fleck of chives put there with masterful deliberation. How the hell did he do that?

Well for one thing, in addition to his experience here in Ireland, where he is rightly regarded as one of our finest chefs, Noel trained extensively abroad, including time spent with Alice Waters in the legendary Chez Panisse restaurant in San Francisco. Noel was brought up on a farm and from an early age learned to treat produce with respect; today, he is still doing exactly that. As he says himself: 'I know what simplicity is. Simplicity means taking raw food, understanding it and cooking it very little.'

Noel has been as Castle Leslie for four years now after running his own restaurant, Trompettes, in Magherafelt in County Derry and engaging in a spot of transatlantic consultancy. While at

Trompettes he elaborated his own range of jams for sale; this has led to the development of a full range of sauces, dips, preserves and oils. These take the Castle Leslie brand not just to the elegant ladies who shop in the multiple delicatessens on the Lisburn Road in Belfast but across the world via online sales from an engaging website.

Noel's travels have greatly influenced his food and he is a firm believer in the philosophy of 'from the garden to the table'. He has brought these influences and this philosophy to the Castle Leslie menus, which are a delight – a hotpot of signature dishes, vegetarian dishes, and of course an internationally themed menu based on locally sourced products. The adventurous should check out the 'eclectic menu', a five-course surprise menu chosen by the chef and reflecting the best produce available today from local markets and their chosen suppliers. Unusually, there is also a laudable wine menu to go with each course.

The Castle has also hosted a series of 'Gourmet Nights' since 2000, the most recent of which were the irreverent 'Shades of Chocolate' and the Paddy's Day 'Celtic Gourmet Night'. Couple this with a lunatic-but-inspired wine list – never before have I heard of a wine that could invite images of ageing lothario Ken Barlow and everybody's favourite thug, Phil Mitchell, to describe it – and one would think that Castle Leslie, with its Beatle connection and boy-genius chef to the fore, could afford to rest on its organic laurels.

But no. Plans are afoot, and this most busy of operations is about to add even more culinary goings-on to its roster. They have taken over the old equestrian centre and are shortly to turn it into a bar and bistro, with the emphasis firmly on all things snack – but good snack. All food sold will be organic, with the idea of heightening interest and awareness among local growers still further and of stimulating excellence across the board. Already, Eurotoques (the European chefs' organisation, which has its own charter, designed to promote the food industry across Europe and uphold the integrity of national cooking) have shown a keen interest in Castle Leslie: they are to host a dinner there in recognition of the place's organic achievements. And if that wasn't enough, they're going to open a cookery school!

CASTLE LESLIE BRAISED SHANK OF LAMB
WITH TRADITIONAL CHAMP AND ROAST VEGETABLES

for the lamb and stock:
4 lamb shanks
1 litre stock (see below)
1 carrot
2 onions
Small bunch rosemary
Small bunch thyme
1 bulb garlic, left whole
Black peppercorns

for the vegetables:
2lb potatoes
Bunch scallions, sliced
Half-lb butter
200ml cream
2 carrots
2 parsnips
1 celeriac
1 small turnip
Olive oil
A little arrowroot
Salt and pepper

To start, make the stock. Trim the shank of lamb, put in an oven tray and add two onions, the bulb of garlic, a carrot, the rosemary and thyme, a few peppercorns and enough water to cover the shanks. Cover with tinfoil and cook in an oven preheated to 200°C for three hours.

In the meantime, cook the potatoes and mash them. Cut the carrots, parsnips, celeriac and turnip into one-inch cubes and season with salt, pepper and olive oil. Roast for fifteen minutes under a hot grill, shaking the pan every few minutes.

To serve, remove the shanks from the stock, reduce the stock, then pass it through a sieve and thicken it with arrowroot.

Roast the shanks in a hot oven until they are crisp on the outside. Warm the cream and add the mashed potatoes, scallions and butter. Stir until hot, then season with salt and pepper. Heat up the vegetables.

Put some champ on a plate and place the shank on top. Sprinkle with roast vegetables and pour over the sauce. *Bon appétit!*

CAVAN

Say the county's name to just about any Irish person, and whether they are from the region or not, invariably you will get the reply, as if as a correction, 'Cyah-van (hey)'. Natives of Cavan are expected to speak like that, while those from outside the county ridicule the county's perceived high state of culchieness, by dint of the way they pronounce the word. It is held that Cavan is the back of beyond – a place of no great interest, especially from a culinary point of view.

While that may once have been true, it is a total fallacy to indulge such a position today. The change has been largely due to one man, a 'wee fella' from the region who has almost singlehandedly put his county and its food on the map. His name is Neven Maguire and he is our 'cheeky, cheery chef', our Jamie Oliver with clothes on.

Neven has become a household name since he first bounced onto our screens four and a half years ago on RTÉ's afternoon magazine programme *Open House*. His easy style and simple approach to food has endeared him to many: his youthful enthusiasm and direct language are engaging – and put an end to the silly prejudices about the county, which are well past their sell-by date.

The day I catch up with him, Neven has just awoken. After a busy Saturday night in his restaurant, the MacNean Bistro in Blacklion, he is about to start his *mise en place* for a lunch of two sittings: some eighty-five people for Sunday lunch and more than thirty already booked in for dinner. Totally unfazed and full of chat, he finds time to accommodate me. Two days before, he cooked a demonstration at the IFEX exhibition in Dublin, appeared on a radio programme and, of course, cooked the Friday night's dinner at the restaurant. He is simply unstoppable.

Young Maguire began his career in the MacNean Bistro, formerly his parents' establishment, at the age of twelve. The restaurant, which lies close to the border, had struggled for many years after opening in 1970, a casualty of the Troubles in the north. In fact, the restaurant was closed from 1973 until 1989. Neven remembers those lean years but also recalls with obvious warmth and pride the ability of his mother, whom he describes as 'a great chef', trained in hotel management and very creative.

In 1989, people were finally beginning to travel again and the restaurant was once more attracting business from neighbouring counties. After a few years in his parents' kitchen, Neven sought work experience elsewhere to develop his skills, his first placement being in the Rankins' then Michelin-starred Belfast restaurant Roscoff (now Cayenne). Neven remembers with pleasure working alongside the likes of Robbie Millar and Eugene O'Callaghan, who turned out stunning food in the glory years of Roscoff, prompting this writer to travel up from Dublin frequently just to eat there.

It wasn't all fun for the young commis chef: the day he started, he was bawled out of it by Rankin for (a) missing his lunch and (b) then eating the bread rolls that were destined for that evening's dinner service. After this rocky start, he stuck with it, often working far beyond the required finishing time simply for the experience. This is a recurring story among dedicated chefs: I once heard of one of Dublin's – nay Ireland's – top chefs whose idea of a holiday each year was to down tools and go to work in the kitchens of three-starred establishments in Lyon as a dishwasher.

Neven would work these long hours Monday to Friday in Roscoff and then return home to Blacklion to cook in the family kitchen. He regards his time in Roscoff as 'brillant' and as being formative in his development.

Following these early inquisitive days, and after qualifying as a chef, Neven continued with his relentless rise to the top. Eschewing holidays, he would head off for places like San Sebastián in Spain for yet more experience – and the attendant influences. Shortly after winning the Baileys 'Young Chef of the Year' award, he gladly accepted as the prize a stint in Luxembourg with Lea Linster, who, he proudly admits, 'taught me so much'. Lea is the only woman ever to win the 'Bocuse d'Or' award – described by Neven as 'the greatest cooking competition in the world'. He subsequently invited her to Cavan, specifically to places like the Organic Centre in Leitrim, where she was amazed by the produce and told Neven to be very grateful that he lived in a county where such magnificent produce was so readily available.

As he brought such experience back to Ireland and matured both in years and as a chef, he reflected on the advice he had received and realised the importance of local produce – a common theme among the chefs of Ireland. These days, 99 percent of his produce is organic and comes from two local producers. He constantly – and modestly – claims that he is only 'as good as the produce he receives', citing the duck, quail, guinea fowl, geese and turkey from Thornhill as the products he rates, and loves to cook in the restaurant.

We laugh as he recounts how these days, so many people bring him what they have shot locally – partridge, pigeon and the like, much more than he can ever use – and how most Mondays he brings the excess up to Dublin, doing the rounds of the capital's finest kitchens and chefs – Guillaume in Guilbaud's, Derry at L'Écrivain, and Kevin at the eponymous Thornton's – and gives them away to them. Neven himself has a great system where he exchanges free dinners to many of his suppliers for their freshly shot game.

Since Neven got the gig with *Open House*, the restaurant has thrived on the ensuing publicity, in addition to the chef's fantastic cooking. He has five bedrooms at the Blacklion, which are now filled on Saturday nights three months ahead as people travel from far and wide to sample the young man's exemplary cooking. Neven is very proud of this but is keen to emphasise that his broadcasting activities in no way hinder his work in the kitchen. People who have made a booking at the restaurant, he says, hear him on the radio, for example, and are concerned that he won't be cooking that night. Not so, he says: if he isn't in the kitchen, 'we don't open'.

He describes his approach to food as new modern Irish cooking: following a recent trip to Thailand, that country's cuisine now features as one of his major influences, taking its place alongside that of France. Like any good chef, he believes in cooking food that is in season; equally, like any good chef, he loves working with fish, which features heavily on his menu. He mentions the presence of many foreigners in the northwest, singling out two Germans who grow spinach just for him, and another

German lady from Belturbet, who makes a goat's cheese called Corleggey.

Neven's enthusiasm is boundless: he is modest to the point of innocence about his own achievements and unstinting in his praise for his staff, his suppliers and the local area. He is trying to get a farmers' market going and was recently invited to attend the first northwest producers' food fair at the Slieve Russell Hotel; it is hoped that this will become an annual event. He describes it as a very professionally staged event; once again, Neven was only happy to cook at it. It was his day off, after all.

As the restaurant is open only four days a week, this leaves him free to attend to such events, as well as, at the beginning of each week, teaching youngsters to cook. We couldn't be having him putting his feet up now, could we?

The pupil eventually becomes the master. In 2001, Neven represented Ireland at the 'Bocuse d'Or' and walked away with the accolade. Now the dedicated young chefs he employs are benefitting from all his knowledge. I wonder if he bites the heads off them for eating the evening's dinner rolls?

This probably shouldn't be called 'shepherd's pie', although that is essentially what it is: the British are quite particular about the distinctions between 'shepherd's pie' (made with lamb) 'cottage pie' (beef) and 'Cumberland pie' (sausage). *Hachis Parmentier* is named in honour of Monsieur Parmentier, who is credited with introducing the potato into France, like Raleigh in Britain. (I can never think of Raleigh without smiling at John Lennon's immortal line: 'He was such a stupid get' – for also introducing tobacco.) I give my recipe for the ultimate comfort fast food, *omelette Parmentière*, on page 157.

In a typical French household, they would collect the leftovers from all the meals during the week – fish, meat, fowl, you name it – and then the father of the family, usually on a Saturday lunchtime, would use a splendid old heavy-duty hand mincer to bind the ingredients together, adding lots of parsley and other herbs and seasonings. The mixture would then be cooked and topped with mashed potato, often with carrot added, to give the dish extra flavour and an eye-catching orange hue. As a twenty-year-old living in France, I was mesmerised at both this genius of economy and the magnificence of flavour that was achieved from such seemingly disparate and potentially clashing ingredients.

In France, *hachis Parmentier* is traditionally accompanied by a fresh green salad. As a rule, the French do not eat cold salads with hot food, but this is one of two exceptions – the other being in Brittany, where they eat a tossed salad with warm and savoury buckwheat pancakes, or galettes, the recipes for which are given on page 219.

Hachis Parmentier is a delicious and comforting dish, and using chicken is a lighter and tasty alternative to beef. Increasingly these days, we are seeing turkey mince in our shops, and this too could be used.

4 breasts of chicken, minced by your butcher
8 medium-sized potatoes, peeled and cut into chunks
2 carrots, peeled and roughly chopped

1 tablespoon tomato purée
1 egg
Glass of milk
1 onion, grated
Large knob of butter
1 clove garlic, finely chopped
2 dried bay leaves
Mixed herbs
Salt and pepper
Glass of white wine
Splash of cream, pinch of nutmeg, 1 tomato, sliced (optional)

Serves 4

For the mashed potato, add the carrots to a saucepan of boiling salted water. After ten minutes, add the peeled potatoes. Boil the carrots and potatoes for another twenty minutes, until soft to the point of a knife. Drain the vegetables and mash with the butter, egg, milk and a little cream if desired. Season to taste with salt and pepper. You could also add a pinch of freshly grated nutmeg. Leave to one side.

For the meat filling, melt a knob of butter in a frying pan, add the onion, bay leaves and garlic and fry until soft, taking care not to let either the onions or the garlic burn. When the onion has softened, add the chicken mince and keep on a medium heat. When the chicken mince is nearly cooked through, add the wine. Season with salt and pepper and add the tomato purée and a generous pinch of mixed herbs. Simmer. Once the chicken mince has been cooked through, remove from the heat and put to one side.

To assemble the dish, place the chicken and all the juices into an ovenproof dish. (You could use one large oven dish to bring to the table or four small bowls for individual servings.) Top with the mashed potato and use a fork to create attactive peaks on the mash. Place in a hot oven for about ten minutes to *gratiner* ('brown'). (To speed the browning process, dot the top of the mash with a couple of small knobs of butter.) If wished, decorate with a few slices of tomato. Serve piping hot, with a green salad.

LEINSTER

LOUTH

Everybody loves the new road. The road I speak of is, of course, the extended M1 from Dublin, which now shaves twenty minutes off the journey to Belfast as it bypasses Drogheda, Dundalk and all those awful roundabouts near Swords and the airport. It can get you to Belfast as fast as the *Enterprise,* meaning that you could leave Dublin on a whim in late afternoon and be in Belfast by seven for an aperitif of Louis Roederer champagne in James Street South before heading up to Cayenne for a meal or up the road a bit further to Taps for one, two or half a dozen tapas.

But one of the real benefits of the new road is how swiftly it gets you to County Louth and more specifically to Carlingford. And Carlingford, it has to be said, situated as it is in the Cooley Peninsula and on the shores of Carlingford Lough, is delightful.

Of course, if you're already living in Dublin, you have any one of half a dozen lovely spots in Wicklow, Wexford and so on within driving distance to go to, and the new-found proximity of Carlingford is just a further bonus. But approaching it from the other direction is one of Ireland's great driving delights: whether for a night out or a weekend away, getting into the car and driving down the A1 from Belfast to Newry, before taking the Omeath 'back road' into the exquisite little medieval village of Carlingford, is a joy.

Omeath was a former Gaeltacht area, one of the last examples of the South Ulster dialect, regrettably destroyed by hordes of northerners who, instead of learning the Irish of the area, displaced it by speaking English to the locals. (This is the origin of the 'no English' rule in today's *Gaeltachtaí* for the hundreds of Irish children who flock there each summer to acquire a grasp of the language.) These days, unless you know your way around, Omeath and Carlingford are rarely explored: most drivers carry on from Newry to Dundalk and thence to Dublin.

Carlingford is one of Ireland's best-preserved medieval towns, founded by the Anglo-Normans in the twelfth century, taking its name from the Norse and meaning 'the fjord of Carlinn'. It became the peninsula's capital; much of the atmosphere and heritage of the place has been retained, and it is an ideal place to wander around and explore.

Despite its piffling size, the town has many pubs – often with traditional music – and a variety of fine restaurants. It sports both gourmet festivals and, in August, an oyster festival, which has always attracted thousands of visitors for the famed delicate oysters of the lough. If Carlingford does not yet enjoy quite the same cachet as Kinsale, with which it is often compared, the fare is truly magnificent, offering as it does excellent beef (as befits the setting of the *Táin Bó Cualigne),* wonderful organic Cooley lamb (on a par with Connemara mountain lamb), mussels, and those aforementioned oysters from Carlingford Lough.

The best of the restaurants include the Oystercatcher, in the middle of town, whose menu features all the foods listed above, as well as lobster and crab. One its more interesting items is a platter of oysters done 'eight ways': a selection of all the different oyster dishes that they offer in their 'oyster corner' on the menu. I certainly 'lorried' into this dish on more than one occasion, thoroughly enjoying it – which is exceptional for me, as generally I prefer my oysters raw, not cooked, ice-cold and with a splendidly realised *sauce mignonette* (the thoughts of which are troubling me so much that I am giving you the recipe for same below).

That oyster platter there certainly taught me to enjoy oysters in a manner other than the traditional. Oysters with blue cheese? With horseradish and smoked salmon? Or even with crispy bacon? At once tempting and shocking, these turned out to be a revelation, and I have since been torn between a half-dozen on the half-shell and a platter such as this. Simply not to be missed.

Main courses at the Oystercatcher retain this deftness of hand, and while the braised shank of mountain lamb is a must-eat delight on at least one of your visits, for every other visit the array of fish on offer is too good to pass up. If you can resist the salmon, the hake or the mussels, then for goodness' sake ignore the fishy 'hot pot' at your peril. Incidentally, the Oystercatcher's butcher is directly opposite the restaurant, should you wish to buy some of the outstanding lamb – or even a hindquarter of the Brown Bull of Cooley – to cook at home.

The area's other famous restaurant (though these days there are many, and I am not for a second forgetting the excellent Kingfisher Bistro) is Ghan House, a serene retreat and for a long time a bastion of good cooking and sumptuous living. They offer gourmet nights seven times a year and great food all year round: they bake their own breads, grow their own herbs in their gardens, and again use the best of local produce – including that to-die-for Cooley lamb. Ghan House offers not only accommodation to pamper yourself with and a terrific restaurant, but also a cookery school on-site, should you wish to develop further your skills with regular courses from top-flight national and international chefs.

County Louth is Ireland's smallest county, home to the twin industrial towns of Dundalk and Drogheda, which are not especially noted for their culinary fame, and so I have dwelt on Carlingford as a place of outstanding natural beauty and great food. Driving there from Belfast gives the feeling of *dépaysement* of which the French are so fond: the feeling of being far from home, a trifle lost, and happy to be so.

But I could not write about County Louth without mentioning a long-established restaurant in the beautiful town of Skerries – with its golden beach – that I gaze at wistfully every time the *Enterprise* roars past it on my frequent trips up to the capital. Yes, I know it's cheating a bit (OK, a lot), because Skerries is firmly within County Dublin, but it's only a matter of minutes from Drogheda. That restaurant is the Red Bank, run by the indefatigable and enigmatic Terry McCoy, he of the silver mane – a dashing figure at food fairs and events and one of Ireland's leading culinary ambassadors. An elegant figure he may cut, all salt and pepper of beard and hair, but boy, can he cook. Again, as befits a seaside village, seafood is proudly to the fore on the wonderful menu, and Terry's menu reflects his non-stop quest to explore and perfect.

Mind you, you must appreciate that I am being both incredibly generous and extremely honest here. We once cooked off against each other at the Abbeyleix Food Fair and he beat me with a fine dish of Kessler pork. Ah, I forgive him.

I've never been a fan of serving Tabasco with oysters, believing it to mask rather than enhance their flavour. I prefer the classic *sauce mignonnette*, with half a dozen on the half-shell, as served in the grand Parisian brasseries such as Bofinger and Les Capucines, with rye bread and Normandy butter. This sauce is also the classic opener in every French household at Christmas for the *réveillon* (the custom of seeing in Christmas or New Year by starting eating at midnight and continuing through the night).

Now, what to drink with it? Best is a simple white wine such as Muscadet or Gros plant. The best variety of the former is that from St Fiacre (St Fiachra!), while the latter, a thin wine made from the *folle blanche* or *picpoul* grape, is said to taste 'infinitely more generous sipped at the quayside at Nantes (its home town) with half a dozen of the crustaceans,' according to Jancis Robinson, if memory serves.

Half a dozen oysters per person
Shallots
30ml red-wine vinegar
Coarse ground black pepper
Crushed ice
Rye bread
Normandy butter

Finely chop the shallots and place in a saucepan with the vinegar, bring to the boil and simmer to reduce. When it is sufficiently reduced (still of a liquid consistency), remove and leave to cool. Season with black pepper if desired.

Open the oysters carefully: wrap your left hand in a tea towel and insert an oyster knife into the muscle of the oyster. Place the opened oysters on the crushed ice (you could add some seaweed – from your fishmonger – for effect), allowing six oysters per person. When ready to eat, spoon a little of the *sauce mignonnette* onto the oyster before consuming. Drink with chilled white wine.

Roast Breast of Turkey with Prunes, Chestnut and Armagnac Stuffing, and Young Potatoes Roasted in Duck Fat with Thyme and Lemon

Speaking of *réveillon*, here's a great Christmas dish. Whether you're having goose or turkey, the most important thing to do is to respect the cooking time. Essentially, the legs take much longer to cook than the breast. This is the main reason for the 'heaviness' associated with Christmas turkey: the more cooked the meat is, the harder it is to digest. While the notion of the festive whole bird on the table is an attractive one, it is really a nonsense in culinary terms. I would heartily recommend that you ask your butcher to separate the breasts from the legs. (There are two added advantages to this approach: the cooking time is greatly reduced, and you can use the carcass to make stock.) If you use the breasts for Christmas lunch, the legs could be done *confit*-style with goose fat and served the following day.

Note the absence of bread from this recipe. Nice as bread stuffing may be, it only adds to the heaviness of the meal.

1 breast of turkey, skin on, per person
    (or you could use a whole turkey)
2 cloves of garlic, crushed
Sea salt
Coarse black pepper
Bunch thyme
1 bag Agen prunes
1 bag *sous-vide* (vacuum-packed) chestnuts
Several strips of smoked bacon or *pancetta*
Bottle of Armagnac
1 tub of duck fat (available from good delis)
New potatoes
    (the quantity will depend on how many guests you have)
1 lemon
Fresh cranberries
Stock made from the turkey carcass
Cranberries to garnish (optional)

Take the breast (or breasts) of turkey and make several incisions in the skin before rubbing the skin all over with the salt, pepper, garlic and half the thyme. While doing this, make the stuffing by simmering the prunes over a low heat with the chopped chestnuts and Armagnac to taste. One or two tablespoons should be enough; you could treat yourself to a glass while cooking! Note that any prune will do but Agen prunes are best, as their flavour is superior and they are free of stones, reducing the work for you.

Place a little butter or oil in a hot pan. When it begins to smoke, place the breasts, skin-side down, in the pan. Brown all over, then turn over and seal on that side too before removing from the pan. Take a sharp knife and make a deep incision in the flesh side down the full length of the breast, to form a deep fold. Spoon the stuffing into the fold and close up. Wrap the meat with the strips of bacon or *pancetta*, to cover the incision. Then place the breasts skin-side down in a roasting tray and put in an oven preheated to around 220 to 250°C.

While the breasts are roasting, parboil the new potatoes, removing them from the cooking water while they are still hard in the centre. About thirty minutes before the end of the cooking time for the turkey breast (using this method, a large breast should take no more than an hour and a quarter), remove it from the oven, place the potatoes all around it with the duck fat and the rest of the thyme, and return to the oven to roast.

After about an hour and ten minutes, remove the breasts and leave in a warm place to rest. (This will make them easier to carve; if they are not fully cooked, they will continue to cook in their own heat. Note that turkey can be eaten pinkish, which makes it much moister, lighter and easier to digest.)

When ready to eat, carve the turkey for serving and place on a platter. (If the turkey is not fully cooked to your liking, return the platter to the oven for a few minutes.) Finely grate lemon zest all over the potatoes, then give them a good stir in the duck fat and thyme (Cilla Black prefers goose fat, trivia fans!) and place in a serving bowl.

If you wish to serve another vegetable with the dish you could consider asparagus, creamed cabbage or Brussels sprouts with cumin, steamed baby carrots or sautéed leeks.

Finally, for a little jus or sauce, you could reduce the stock you made with the turkey carcass. Then deglaze the pan in which you sealed the turkey breast with a glass of white wine and add this to the reduced stock. When the liquid is of a syrupy consistency, thicken it – and create a sheen – with a few knobs of butter, and season with salt and pepper. You could also stir in a little redcurrant jelly if desired. Serve the jus in a sauce boat. For a final touch, garnish the turkey platter with some sprigs of cranberries.

MEATH

Meath is one of those counties which I spend a fair bit of time travelling through on my way from Dublin to Belfast, or vice versa, on those rare occasions when I travel by car, but I rarely stop there. To the outsider, Meath gives the impression that it might be one of those curious counties where little appears to happen and where places that people recommend to you have often, sadly, vanished by the time you catch up with them.

If you turn off the main roads into leafy and lost byways, however, there is an unsung world of hidden-Ireland country houses and hotels, chief of which must be the Station House in Kilmessan. I can hear Ireland give a collective groan as I once again manage to find an excuse to mention trains and railways, but really, how can I ignore a first-class hotel which is built in an old railway station and whose bridal suite is in an original signal box?

The accommodation there is unbridled luxury, if you'll excuse the intended pun; the Station House also boasts a spacious and delightful restaurant. I will resist the overwhelming temptation to state that it's *railly* good. Featuring lamb from the area as well as salmon from the River Boyne, it combines olde-worlde charm (and railway chic) with modern cooking. It is also within easy reach of Dublin, for a Saturday night of pampering or a weekend away from the big smoke. They say, too, that if you have a drink outside in the still air, you can hear the echo of the last train, which passed through in 1963. OK, I'll stop now.

People speak highly of the Hudson Bistro in Navan, of Catty Ned's in Dunshaughlin (which may or may not be closed), of an excellent Indian whose name no one can remember in Virginia, and of somewhere equally anonymous in Bettystown on the coast, but like so much of Meath, these establishments are either far from anywhere or else in sleepy hamlets.

Meath is famous chiefly for its rock and pop concerts at Slane Castle (best visited by helicopter, if you're going, in order to avoid the traffic back to Dublin afterwards), but the county also has an agricultural pedigree and quietly gets on with the business of growing and supplying vegetables for the rest of the country. It also boasts one of the most surreal sights in the country. On the site of Largo Foods, makers of the Mr Perri brand, is a herd of buffalo. Now, Mr Perri makes the wacky 'Hunky Dorys Buffalo Flavour Thick & Chunky Potato Chips', and in a promotional move, Mr. Perri in his wisdom imported buffalo into Ireland and established a buffalo farm on the ranch, er, site. Chances are that you'll bump into one of these hairy beasts when you're driving round the countryside. The meat – which, by the way, is absolutely delightful, combining the satisfaction of a steak with the lightness and flavour of other exotic meats – is now to be found on some of the local menus. Buffalo steaks can be bought at Largo Foods HQ, although they are often frozen: the meat is not being actively promoted by the company as yet. Here then is a recipe for grilling buffalo; the marinade could be used for other exotic meats, such as kangaroo, alligator or even iguana.

I have always liked working with exotic meats such as ostrich, kangaroo and buffalo, many of which have become commonplace in Ireland. Ostrich are farmed in County Tipperary, and the exquisite Finnebrogue venison farmed in County Down is now available all over Ireland.

Some of these meats need a little help prior to cooking because they can be rather tough. When I was presented with the challenge of cooking buffalo for the first time, I called upon a marinade which I have been using for years, which has the effect of tenderising whatever meat it is applied to. This marinade will also work on a simple steak or the increasingly popular turkey steak.

Buffalo steaks (one per person)
Peanut oil
1 bottle of Kikkoman soy sauce
6 (or more) cloves of garlic,
    skins left on, crushed with the flat of a knife
Bay leaves
1 onion, peeled and sliced
Cracked black pepper
Fresh ginger, roughly sliced
Parsley and coriander, roughly chopped

Place the buffalo steaks or other meats in a bowl and pour enough oil over them to coat them. Splash the steaks liberally with soy sauce and toss them so that the oil and soy mixture has come in contact with every part of them. Add the bay leaves and garlic, onion, parsley, coriander and ginger. Mix well and place in the fridge. Turn frequently. Make the marinade as long in advance as you can – at least an hour.

When about to cook the meat, heat the pan and remove the steaks from the marinade, leaving most of it behind (except for any bits of garlic, which will add to the flavour). You could spoon the oil-and-soy mix over the cooked meats before serving.

Chermoula is a basic recipe for most fishes that appear in Moroccan recipes, whether they are fried, cooked in tagines, or stuffed and baked in the oven. The sauce can also accompany barbecued fish: it would go especially well with fillet of tuna, swordfish, shark or indeed red snapper. *Chermoula* is one of the tastiest sauces around, featuring great bunches of coriander and liberal doses of garlic, sweet and fiery peppers, and olive oil. It can be prepared in advanced and stored in a jar in the fridge.

    Large bunch of coriander
    Sea salt
    4 garlic cloves, peeled
    Half a glass of water
    2 or 3 red peppers, roasted
    2 tablespoons paprika
    2 tablespoons cayenne pepper
    1 hot red chilli
    1 tablespoon cumin
    Juice of 1 lemon
    250ml olive oil

Traditionally, *chermoula* is made with a mortar and pestle, but a great result can be achieved with a modern food mixer: just pulse all the ingredients, rather than mixing them, to form a smooth paste. If using with fish, cover a whole fish inside and out with the mixture before roasting or barbecuing.

Naturally, I thought that everyone had at one time or another driven to Clare to visit the house where *Father Ted* was filmed: a comedic shrine that should be every Irish person's mecca. No? Well, harrumph. If you had, and you'd travelled from the north of the country, you would probably have driven through the village of Glasson; you may even have dropped in to one of its delightful hostelries.

It was my dear friend Alain Storme, Meath's champion stud farmer, who first alerted me to Glasson's charms. It is an extremely handsome village, festooned with flowers, and with much to recommend it as a place to stop off on your way from here to there. Dotted with a fair number of welcoming pubs and restaurants, such as the Glasson Village restaurant, its glory has to be the magnificent Wineport. This establishment, dedicated to food and wines, in an idyllic setting in the heart of Ireland, also offers sinful accommodation in ten indulgent rooms. I know: I stayed there. There are jets in the shower for the backs of your knees. The mirrors don't steam up. The floors are warm.

But it isn't just all these pampering luxuries, nor indeed the creative menus of chef Feargal O'Donnell, or the exhaustive wine lists (which feature, among other things, some very tempting champagnes) that set the Glasson Village apart from others in Ireland. It is its unique setting on the edge of Ireland's most peaceful inland waterway, the inner lakes of Lough Ree. Established in February 1993 by Ray Byrne and Jane English, it describes itself as Ireland's first 'wine hotel': each of the ten rooms has a different wine theme. It also has a very grand Taittinger Champagne Lounge, which is used for wine tastings.

Although it is easy to get to the Wineport from the rest of the country via Athlone, I can think of no finer way of approaching it – either for dinner or for a longer stay – than from the water. You can catch a boat at the town jetty in Athlone for a trip which is peaceful yet invigorating, with the promise of fine food and wine on arrival at the Wineport's own jetty.

Wine, as you may have gathered, is very much to the fore here in Westmeath: it has been established through research that 'Wineport' is in fact the original name for the townland. It was St Ciaran, way back in 542 AD, who brought wine from France to Limerick, and from there up the Shannon to Wineport, where the barrels were rolled down to Ballyciaran. Ciaran, obviously a busy man, later established a monastery at Clonmacnoise.

Elsewhere in County Westmeath is another wine connection. I first met Paddy Keogh when he was a commandant in the Irish army and was indulging his love of wines by selling them via his fledgling company Wines Direct, working out of Mullingar in Westmeath. Paddy walked nonchalantly (in so far as any army officer can walk nonchalantly) into my Dublin restaurant Shay Beano one midweek afternoon with a case full of interesting wines, and, as I stood to attention, proceeded to pour and to talk with a rare passion about his 'cadets'.

The first wine Paddy ever treated me to was a Château Sarail du Guillimière, a Bordeaux that was then practically unknown in Ireland, but one of which I was quickly to imbibe litres. Pleasant and unassuming, with a price tag that no one could baulk at, it made for one of those classic 'house wines' that any caring establishment would be proud to stand over.

This Bordeaux was typical of the type of wine Paddy was to sell in large quantities over the next few years as his company grew. (He subsequently left the army to develop the business fulltime.) I was so impressed that I brought the wine (and Paddy) first to the evergreen Elephant and Castle in Dublin's Temple Bar and then to Fitzers on Dawson Street, two premises which are now Paddy's biggest customers.

Today, Wines Direct is a nationwide company: 75 percent of its trade is still restaurant-orientated, while 25 percent comes from mail order by means of the company's excellent website, *www.winesdirect.ie*. Paddy is as enthusiastic as ever – and still on the hunt for 'charming and refreshing wines, as distinct from blockbusters', as he puts it. He firmly believes in good research and says that it is essential to go to the vineyard in pursuit of wines of which he wants his customers to say: 'I could drink a bottle of that.'

Spiralling prices for Bordeaux wines have meant, of course, that Bordeaux is no longer the sole region the company deals with. Many of Paddy's more charming wines now come from the south of France, Languedoc especially, rather than from the Gironde, where the most famous Bordeaux wines are produced. Others – perhaps surprisingly, given the company's long association with French wines – come from Australia, where Paddy has made several forays in recent years.

When leaving Glasson, or on your way from Mullingar westwards, do stop in the town of Athlone. Here you may enjoy a pint in Sean's Bar, reckoned to be the oldest in the land (and from where, Ray Byrne of Wineport says, you will always be able to organise a boat up to them). For eats, look no further than the Left Bank Bistro, a joyous restaurant that makes most of the rest of Ireland feel jealous and deprived.

The Wineport have generously given me one of their delicious recipes, a celebration of the local lamb and the wine that is their raison d'être. My thanks to Ray Byrne and Feargal O'Donnell.

2 racks of lamb, French-trimmed by your butcher

for the crust:
150g breadcrumbs
2 sprigs fresh mint
2 sprigs rosemary
2 sprigs parsley
2 cloves garlic
Rind of 1 lemon
4 tablespoons olive oil
4 tablespoons sweet mustard

for the dauphinoise:
2 heads celeriac, peeled and roughly chopped
1 pint cream
2 cloves garlic, chopped
1 bottle of inexpensive red burgundy (or any pinot noir wine)
Salt and pepper

Serves 4

for the crust:
Blend together all the ingredients except the mustard.

for the rack of lamb:
Seal the lamb in hot oil and leave to rest. Brush liberally with mustard and coat generously with the crust mixture. Cook in a preheated oven at 175°C for about twenty-five minutes for pink, or about forty-five minutes for well-done.

for the dauphinoise:
Heat the wine in a saucepan to almost boiling point and cook the celeriac in it until soft (about ten minutes). Strain off most of the wine. Add the cream and crushed garlic, and season well. Boil

until the cream thickens, then purée in a blender until smooth. Check the seasoning.

to serve:
After roasting, allow the lamb to rest for ten minutes. Spoon the celeriac mixture onto warm plates, then carve the lamb into cutlets. Serve with some crunchy green vegetables and a little mint jelly.

LONGFORD

Writing a book such as this, and telling people about it, frequently prompts the typical retort to its county-by-county nature from some of my more evil acquaintances: 'Even Longford?' It is true that the county has practically no reputation for food and is one of those places where, should you need to find a place to dine, you will almost inevitably end up in a Chinese restaurant. Indeed, looking up a website for eating out in Longford reveals in the 'international' section no fewer than seven Chinese restaurants and takeaways, one Indian – and nothing else.

Longford is, I confess, a difficult one. Almost smack-dab in the middle of Ireland, it isn't our top culinary destination. A plan that I had to keep back a description of boxty for this one and maybe a wee recipe to go with it is now scuppered because boxty isn't, as I'd believed, indigenous to the area but is in fact more typical of border counties. Ah well, sure I'll get you again.

There seems to be no shortage of things to do in Longford, but eating out isn't one of them. The tourist board's slogan 'Easy to reach, hard to leave' may well be true, but the visitor may be advised to confine his or her eating to 'good old-fashioned Irish fare' of the kind frequently boasted of on the various Longford websites. I felt it to be a fruitless exercise to try to find top-class or top-quality restaurants in an area of Ireland that is so far from any urban centre, since it would prove difficult for them to survive, even if they could find willing bums to put on seats.

Instead, let's look at food products. The outstanding product of Longford town itself is the delightful Torc Truffles, which now grace many a fine table in Ireland and abroad. These hand-made chocolates are produced from only natural ingredients here in the very heart of Ireland. The range is large, boasting selections of chocolates and the superior champagne truffles, as well as recent additions such as cakes, handmade biscuits and chutneys.

Torc Truffles have been made in Longford since 1994, a creation of Ruth McGarry Quinn and her husband, Joe. There are other Irish chocolates of various quality on the market, but Torc

Truffles are exclusive and for the discerning: they are only available in small, specialist outlets. It speaks volumes about a truffle product such as this that one of the largest markets for it is Belgium, home of fine chocolate and the truffle itself.

But soft, what is this? Torc Truffles have gone one step further and opened a café at Ballymahon Street in Longford, right in the heart of the midlands. The place is one of those combinations of café and chocolate shop that would remind you of the likes of Bernachon in Lyon. Well, perhaps not quite, he grinned, but it is unique, and has been voted by *Food and Wine Magazine* as one of the top ten cafés in the country, outside Dublin.

The café offers a fine selection of specialist coffees, lunchtime items such as wraps, salads and sandwiches, and a wide variety of club sandwiches, not to mention Irish favourites such as scones and jam – and, of course, the famous truffles can be bought here loose. See that now?

When I was a nipper, one of my favourite treats was potato apple – which sounded as weird to me then as it probably does to you reading this now. No matter, it was utterly delicious and continues to be a Belfast treat, found for example in the Friday market at St George's Market in the city.

Apples
150g plain flour
500g potatoes, cooked and mashed
Salt
30g butter

Mix the flour into the (lump-free) mash until you have a workable dough. Cut it in half and roll each half out into a circle.

Peel and dice the apples and cook them briefly in a pan with a little butter and sugar. They must remain firm. Spread the apple around the first circle of dough and then place the second circle on top, sealing it with your thumbs.

Cook on both sides on a griddle pan for about five minutes per side or until you can smell the apples – which indicates that they are cooked. Serve hot, with lashings of butter!

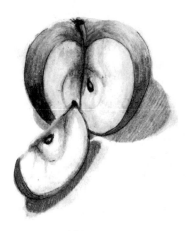

OFFALY

So what's from Offaly? Well, as any fule no, Tullamore Dew, made in the small county town of Tullamore, has long flown the flag for this county in the near-heart of Ireland – since 1829, in fact. But as usual, my brief was more the food than the drink, and it was the promise of bacon 'like it used to be' that drew me to Birr, to investigate the phenomenon that is Rudd's bacon, and to cook and taste it.

I assumed we'd be in another typical Irish town, far from anywhere in particular, the usual main street with its haberdashers, clothes shops, gaudy doors and walls, umpteen pubs, at that time not yet sporting their Smokers' Union meetings outside – and of course the eventual Chinese restaurant where we'd eat because we didn't yet know of anywhere else. Hopefully there'd even be a great handwritten sign somewhere like the one I'd seen in Rath Luirc outside a shop of no fixed retail persuasion that read 'Opening soon with a MASSIVE closing down sale.'

But not a bit of it: Birr is a neat, tidy and pristine little place, an attractive Georgian town, no less. Among its many attractions (and they are many), it has the Seffin Stone, also known as the navel of Ireland, or *umbilicus Hiberniae*, as well as some fine shopfronts that are so outstandingly pretty, they've probably won awards worldwide at the annual shopfronts awards ceremony. Furthermore, it boasts Birr Castle, a castle among castles, a splendid example of seventeenth-century architecture, and well worth a visit. Ah, who am I kidding? Skip the architecture: I tell you, it's got the tastiest wild watercress growing around it, thanks to the wild peatland and good old St Brendan, and it makes a great soup in the time it takes to boil a pot of water; you can always feign interest in castle-type things after you've supped.

Next door to the castle, in the sensibly named Castle Street, are Spinners Townhouse and Bistro, where we spent a more than comfortable night in their magnificent rooms. The Bistro, which we discovered at breakfast, was to prove as nifty as the accommodation, with the admirable slogan 'Buy local and think global.'

We had been too late on arrival that first night for the Bistro and ate in the first Chinese restaurant that we found – which was, true to the form of modern Ireland, absolutely brilliant. It offered Thai as well as Chinese specialities and sold not just bottles of Tiger beer but also Tsing Tsao (the beer that, just when you think you've learned how to pronounce it like a native, mysteriously changes pronunciation from one speaker to the next) and Singha, the refreshingly crisp Thai beer with a nose like an Alsace *edelzwicker* and a growl on the throat that quenches the most needy of thirsts. The restaurant's name has long since passed into wherever restaurant names go when you've forgotten them, but it was just around the corner from Spinners. You'll find it.

Those were my first surprises, the first preconceptions turned upside down. The other came when, on leaving the townhouse, I was confronted by an amazing but increasingly common sight in contemporary Ireland: a terrace of about a dozen houses that seemed to have an African family living in every one.

Straightaway I was intrigued by the great sense of camaraderie: men, women and children were leaning over each other's hedges and chattering away excitedly, with that typical African friendliness evident in their sweeping gestures and broad smiles. When I too leaned a bit further in the direction of the hedges and ear-wigged, I instantly recognised the language as Lingala, that beautiful, mellifluous tongue, spiced with a heavily accented French and peppered with Belgicisms, that marks out citizens of the modern Congo. Wonder what the Lingala for 'nosey bugger' is?

Quite apart from the dramatic chatter in the fresh air, there was much toing and froing from all of the front doors, giving the impression that all these people lived in one big house, much like the Beatles' abode in *Help!*, where the individual doors led into a single, massive living room. And like the dwelling of 'the four lads who shook the world', it looked as if there was great fun to be had indoors: maybe music, maybe singing, surely dancing, Congolese rumba on the sound system, soukous to shake your body to? Bisso na Bisso, the young Congolese rap band? And food too?

I was just beginning to wonder if there were any smells emanating from the row of houses when I was called away, but the experience gave me pause to wonder if, like in Dublin, ethnic shops, where ingredients could be easily found for typical Central African fare, had followed in the wake of our new fellow-citizens?

For this reason I offer the simple recipe for *poulet à la muambe* (chicken with tomato-and-peanut sauce) below, the delicious Congolese stew I was taught by a friend from Kinshasa, who struggled to make it for me a few years back, when there were few other black faces around – and no ingredients to be found, as there are today. And *foufou*, the polenta-like staple which accompanies the dish, which at the time sounded to me like a name for a pet poodle. I hope Irish people will try this most satisfying of dishes, with its hot sauce on the side, and enjoy, with a twelve-inch groove of Seigneur Tabu Ley Rochereau in the background. I hope too that this printing of it will put a smile on the face of any members of the Congolese quarter of Birr, puzzled by the spiky-haired, staring *mundele* of late July 2003.

But now to Rudd's. Rudd's is the brainchild of Prue & David Rudd and Family. The company was established in 1973 but in 1985 a range of products appeared bearing the Rudd brand. The company, which was originally situated in Nenagh in County Tipperary, recently relocated to an ultra-modern plant in Birr, where they now produce sausages, hams, bacon, black and white puddings, and a huge range of carefully elaborated traditional recipes, unique seasonings and hands-on curings.

There is simply nothing like their bacon products. You know as soon as the bacon hits the tongue that this is a product rich in flavour and to be savoured. From the instant it hits the pan, the look, and the effect on the olfactory senses, is incomparable. There is no water oozing out here, no white scum adhering to the flesh, since all Rudd's products come from pigs fed on natural rations, and they contain absolutely no artificial colouring agents or flavour enhancers.

The puddings, the sausages, the rashers – these are all wonderful, but for my part I love working with bacon chops and joints. There is something very earthy about such food, and I love to play with it, taking inspiration from the potees (hearty stews) of the Auvergne or our own bacon and cabbage, and naturally the Alsace masterpiece choucroute, that study in pork.

RUDD'S BACON CHOPS WITH MASHED POTATO
MUSTARD CABBAGE AND SHALLOT VINAIGRETTE

Working with a Rudd's bacon chop was a complete pleasure: I seem to recall making a potato and celeriac rosti to underpin it and settling the bacon chop on top of some quickly cooked spinach. A product such as this needs to be celebrated, highlighted, pushed to the fore, its accompaniments politely, firmly and rightly in the background. Given that Rudd's produce a variety of meats and meat products, in this recipe I have used their black pudding as a foil for the chops, with mashed potatoes.

    4 Rudd's bacon chops
    Peanut oil
    Sherry vinegar
    Sprigs of fresh thyme
    Two tomatoes, diced
    Meaux mustard
    Glass of milk
    Fresh parsley, roughly chopped
    Three shallots
    8 large potatoes
    1 small black-pudding ring
    Irish butter
    1 savoy cabbage or local green cabbage, shredded
    Salt and pepper

To make the vinaigrette, combine three parts oil with one part vinegar. For this dish, combine six tablespoons of oil with two of vinegar, add a pinch of salt and cracked black pepper and whisk thoroughly. Finally, add a generous quantity of the parsley. You can either finely chop the shallots and add these to the sauce or if, like meself, you are supremely lazy – and also to give a more inter- esting texture – grate them directly into the dressing using a cheese grater. Mix well, and adjust the seasoning.

Peel and boil the potatoes. While they are cooking, oil the bacon chops on both sides, add salt and pepper, and the sprigs of thyme, snapped in half to help release the oils. Place the chops on a grill pan or frying pan and cook on both sides over a medium heat for about five minutes a side. In another pot, cook the cabbage for no more than four minutes, then drain and keep warm, with a little of the cooking water retained.

When the potatoes are cooked, drain and pulverize them in Ye Olde Irish manner with a potato masher – or a wooden spoon. Add a little milk and a knob of butter, then season and add some parsley. Finally, open the black pudding, break the filling into the mash and leave on the heat to cook, stirring regularly. The point of using a small pudding is to give just a hint of it through the mash.

Finish off the cabbage by stirring in a knob of butter and a generous dollop of Meaux mustard. Season with plenty of pepper, which really suits cabbage, but go easy on the salt as there is already some in the butter.

If you want to try one of those tall, architectural presentations, take a wide pastry ring, spoon some of the mash mixture onto the plate, filling the ring, then remove it, leaving a perfect little round of mash. Carefully place some of the cabbage on top of that, then finally place one of the chops on top of the cabbage. Add any remaining pan juices to the vinaigrette before giving a final stir and spooning some of it over the glistening chop. Garnish with the tomatoes. This dish is great with a glass of an Irish beer.

I've always felt drawn to the Congo region in the heart of Africa, mainly because of the influence its music has had on me. I would like to suggest a dish that the people eat, a true taste of 'over there', to enjoy with your rumba, soukous and *mutuashi* music – the classic dance rhythms of the Congo.

In the Congo, chicken has long been considered a luxury dish: it was traditionally served to guests, village elders, in-laws and others. Every family had a small farmyard and a cockerel or hen was 'sacrificed', usually in front of the guest (as a proof of the meat's freshness). The humble chicken has thus acquired a symbolic value in relation to hospitality: serving it shows that you esteem youor guests. Even if you were to serve, for example, an expensive fish, like snapper, lobster or tuna, that cost three times as much as chicken, your Congolese guest would feel insulted that you had not offered him a chicken from your own backyard!

The practice of cooking a chicken for guests has spread to the urbanized areas, in a rare example of the town learning its manners from the countryside. Despite the advent of battery-reared chickens, these are still looked upon with disdain and are not suitable for this dish. A quality, sizeable chicken 'in good health' is the recommendation, and we should seek a free-range or organic bird to use in this dish, even if you do not go as far as slaughtering it in your home.

The dish is traditionally served with a staple called '*foufou*' (or Creole rice). *Foufou* is said to resemble polenta, with various provinces of the Congo (like the Italians) preferring a hard or soft variation of it. The dish was traditionally made from a combination of corn and cassava (manioc) flours, but the difficulty of obtaining the latter, as well as the acquisition of a more sophisticated palate by expatriate Congolese, has prompted the use of semolina instead. Essentially, a thick paste is made and served immediately. It is fairly bland but an excellent foil to the chicken sauce; it may be given a lift by addition of 'piment' sauce.

These recipes are traditionally handed down orally from mother to daughter: women do all the cooking in the Congo and no precise recipes are available. The success of the dish thus depends on the skill of the cook.

for the chicken:
1 good-sized chicken
1 large onion
2 or 3 large tomatoes, peeled, deseeded and sliced
Tomato purée
Salt
3 large tumblers of chicken stock
Selection of herbs
Three or four tablespoonfuls peanut butter or peanut paste
Oil (ideally, palm oil, if you can find a bottle)

for the piment sauce:
Red and green chillis
Lemon juice
Oil
Sage and mint
1 large onion

Serves 4 to 6

Quarter the chicken, leaving the legs whole, and the wings on the breasts. Brown the pieces all over in a little oil, remove from the pot or pan and place to one side. Sauté the sliced onions in the oil, add the tomatoes, tomato purée and stock, and return the chicken pieces to cook in this mixture. At this point, fresh herbs, such as sage, mint and Provence herbs may be freely added, and the dish should be seasoned with salt and pepper. Leave to cook until the chicken is tender. Towards the end of cooking, add the peanut butter (or peanut paste) and leave to simmer, stirring frequently.

To make the piment sauce, deseed and chop red and green hot chillis and either chop them finely in a blender or use the traditional mortar and pestle. Add a finely chopped onion and aromatic herbs and blend these with the chillis. Then add a little freshly squeezed lemon juice and mix well. Serve on the side in a ramekin.

110

I have been extolling the virtues of *sauce chien* for many a long year now because (a) I think it's a damn fine, tasty sauce and (b) it's extremely versatile and can be used to enliven all kinds of meats or fish, sandwiches and salads, hot or cold. I also cling to the belief that I might be recognised as the discoverer of one of the last great unplundered cuisines, that of the French West Indies, from which this sauce comes, as the supermarkets squeeze their last cent out of the bastardised Thai-Moroccan-Mexican mishmashes that they have foisted upon us. (From which Muslim hamlet did 'couscous with pork curry' emerge?)

Mind you, I haven't had too much success with *sauce chien:* maybe it's because of the name – and probably also because I prattle on too much about it. So let me state here in print that it has nothing whatsoever to do with dogs. Rather, the *'chien'* in the title probably refers to the bite it possesses from the hot chillis used in its preparation.

It is the equivalent of the hot pepper sauce found throughout the English-speaking Caribbean – of which the best is Matouk's from Trinidad and the worst, in my opinion, is the one found everywhere in Barbados, the horrible yellow American-mustardy, not-quite-at-the-races type. But these are all industrially made sauces, whereas in Martinique and Guadeloupe *sauce chien* is always made domestically or in a restaurant kitchen by hand – and is all the better for it. Naturally, variants abound, but I am pleased to present a pretty good catch-all recipe below.

This is a sauce I always have made up in quantity in my fridge: it's quick, cheap and simple to make, stores for an eternity and, best of all, is light on the old waistline, since its main ingredient is water. You can serve it with anything, and having it about turns the most pedestrian of leftovers into something deliciously tasty in seconds.

These quantities will make enough for six people, but you can multiply the quantities and store the result in a sealed jar in the fridge.

111

1 small ramekin of finely chopped chives
1 bouquet of finely chopped parsley
4 whole cloves, crushed and roughly chopped
2 cloves of garlic, thinly sliced
2 shallots, diced
1 red Scotch-bonnet chilli pepper, seeded and chopped
2 tablespoons of fresh thyme.
1 onion, finely diced or grated
5 tablespoons of olive or peanut oil
Juice of one lemon
1 large cup of very hot, but not boiling, water

Serves 6

The preparation is simplicity itself: heat the oil gently in a saucepan and fry the garlic, the shallots and one of the tablespoons of thyme. Do not allow to colour. Put all the other ingredients into a jar and mix well. Pour the hot water on top of these ingredients, then add the oil mixture from the saucepan. Transfer the lot into whatever jar or bottle you are going to keep it in and put the lid on. Shake the container vigorously for about thirty seconds. Keep it in the fridge for at least twelve hours before use. It's great with chicken, pork, kid goat, swordfish, steamed cod, prawns and mussels. *En nou ale!*

LAOIS

There are three things that spring to mind when I think of Laois – two of them mentioned elsewhere in this book. One is 'The Lads of Laois', a 'man's reel' that is demanding on the fingers, ideally suited to fiddle and banjo, and great fun and satisfying to play. Another is the Abbeyleix Food Fair, now sadly defunct. And of course there is the famous Morrison's pub, again in Abbeyleix, which dates from the eighteenth century and is a favourite stopping-off point for snacks and beer when driving 'down the country'. Naturally, it has spawned many imitators, Morrison's in Belfast being the most blatant copy, though they have recently given up on the 'Oirish' atmosphere and embraced a more contemporary café look, with loud recorded noise for the youngsters.

What you don't expect from a Midlands county such as Laois is a great Indian restaurant, the Kingfisher in Portlaoise – though it is typical of modern Ireland that surprises such as this can turn up in the most unlikely of settings. In fact, I have long had a love-hate relationship with Indian restaurants in this country.

The one complaint you can never make about an Indian restaurant is that you left the place hungry: it seems to me that even a few mouthfuls of this food tends to fill a body. What do they put in it? The starters are often smaller versions of the main courses, the main courses rarely vary from establishment to establishment, the way in which the dishes are cooked is very similar from one restaurant to the next, yet people flock to them. I have long held that Indian food has an addictive quality. The food, unlike many Mediterranean dishes, cannot be eaten cold, and there is thus a tendency to gobble it, lest it go cold in front of you. This only increases the heaviness that you feel afterwards. Washing it down with beer serves only to bloat you further, as the rice and naan breads absorb the liquid. I often feel uncomfortable at the end of an Indian meal, or else make a conscious decision to eat only half of the food that is put in front of me.

The last few years have seen a number of 'new-wave' Indian restaurants open around the country. These places, which include

Poppadum and Vermilion in Dublin, offer not just a lighter, more enlightened approach to the food but also – at last – a regional one. As a result, the menus often depart from the norm of *jal ferezis,* kormas, *ghoshts* and bhunas. Restaurants such as these have discouraged patrons from drinking beer – even Kingfisher and Cobra – with the food.

They also serve to underscore a worrying north-south trend: Indian restaurants in the north tend to be very poor. There is no equivalent of the Dublin restaurants mentioned above, meaning that most of the Indians in, say, Belfast consist of the usual menu, the usual outdated sitar music and the usual flock wallpaper. Worse, the meat used is generally from frozen and, in the case of the ersatz chicken, of extremely dubious quality. Lately I have noticed in certain Indian takeaways the use of the cheapest form of rice that can be found: it is barley-like and unpalatable.

The difference south of the border is palpable: the second you bite into something in most of Dublin's leading Indian restaurants, you are aware of better ingredients, better cooking and superior saucing. This quality has made itself felt throughout the Republic, which is why great Indian restaurants there can be found in the most remote parts of the country. Would that the trend would spread to the six counties!

The Kingfisher in Portlaoise, a partner restaurant to the excellent Shalimar in Dublin's South Great George's Street, is one of the new Indian restaurants that are setting high standards in that sector. To me it is scarcely credible that such a restaurant can exist in a town of ten-thousand-plus people when I can barely get a decent garlic naan at home in Belfast. I can't be flitting down to Portlaoise every time I fancy a *boti shashlik* or *murgh gosht!*

Midlands cuisine has made great strides in recent years, with the result that stopping off in towns such as Portlaoise, where only a few short years ago you really wouldn't have bothered, is a pleasure, a thrill even. In fact, you would now make a point of going there to eat rather than treating it as a stopping-off place on your way to somewhere else. The fact that restaurants such as the Kingfisher offer such excellence and attention to detail speaks volumes about the confidence the business sector has in modern Ireland, its people and their palates.

I was in Turin at the time of the outbreak of the first Gulf war and spent a week there, eating every night in different friends' houses, usually eight-course banquets, as only the Italians know how. One of these served three different kinds of octopus in completely different ways! In between courses, we argued long into the night about the computer-game war scenes being televised.

I spent the last day in the city centre alone, forcing myself to go to a restaurant for lunch for what I convinced myself was a little R&D for my own establishment. I love the ordering system in an Italian restaurant, where you first order a *primo* and eat it before ordering a *secondo* – and only if you want. I would hate to be on the receiving end of that in a kitchen, but they all handle it admirably.

It suited me that day, for I wasn't too hungry after my various octopus, risotto and pasta orgies – or feeling too clever after a week of wine and grappa. I began with the city's speciality, *agnolotti,* which the rest of Italy and the world refers to as ravioli, and a bottle of my one true love: Sassicaia. The staff stared in astonishment at this lone diner quaffing a whole bottle of this relatively expensive – even in its home country – wine while giving a passable impression of a person who was about to pass on.

I couldn't decide on a *secondo.* I didn't want meat or fish and stared at the menu for the time it took to drink another glass of Sassicaia. Then I saw it. My wee dish. *Perfetto.* Fried eggs with shaved white truffles and a little olive oil. Perfectly cooked, with runny eggs, lashings of black pepper and truffles grated at your table. I ate with gusto. Here's how you do it.

4 eggs
Truffles
Olive oil
Black pepper
A second mortgage

115

Pour a little olive oil into a frying pan and heat over a medium flame. Call the bank manager on speakerphone and discuss the mortgage while cooking the eggs. Break the eggs into the pan and leave to cook. If you want them a little more cooked, don't turn them over or spoon oil over them: place them in the pan under the grill for thirty to forty seconds, and that will do the job.

Place the eggs on the table, still in the pan. Liberally grate black pepper over them (which looks fabulous) and then shave the truffles onto them. To save money, use an ordinary cheese grater: there's an ideal slit at the back. Pour a large glass of Sassicaia or Solaia and smile expansively.

Your bank manager will probably charge an arrangement fee too, so factor that in.

KILDARE

As I was a-goin' the road to Athy
I saw an oul' petticoat hangin' to dry.
I took off my oul' britches and hung them nearby
To keep the oul petticoat warm.

County Kildare was always well known to me in song, long before I ever went there. The above verse, which amused me for many a year, comes from Gay and Terry Woods' album *The Woods Band*, now unfortunately long out of print. I listened to it ad nauseam in the seventies. Before that, I loved 'The Curragh of Kildare' by the Johnstons (pre-Mick Moloney and Paul Brady), which was the opening track on Side Two of a long-deleted Marble Arch album called *The Travelling People*. (The eponymous track, an Irish number one, was blared out of the single record shop in Falcarragh in Donegal where I spent the summer of 1968. The banner across the shop's window was a common sight in 1960s Ireland and bore a legend that I remember with fondness: 'Records are cheaper in Ireland'. And they were: thirty of the old shillings, as opposed to the UK's price of 39/11.)

The inland county of Kildare is synonymous with the race-courses in the Curragh, Punchestown and Naas. It's a lush county with lots of well-tended plains, golf courses and elegant gardens, such as the Tully Japanese Gardens near Kildare town – as well as plenty of great big castles.

Sadly, for a long time now all I've seen of the county is the view from the train, on my way to Cork, Limerick or Galway. This is not so bad: I've had surprisingly good meals on the train, and am generally on my second bottle of Bordeaux by the time we hit Kildare. I find it remarkable that in Ireland we can still get something half-decent to eat on our trains: maybe it's because so many of them are still so slow. The menu on the much speedier *Enterprise* to Belfast is currently woeful. Several attempts have been made to refine it, with recipes from Paul Rankin and Robbie Millar, but these efforts have failed because, in the absence of those two chefs, the execution of the dishes was never satisfactory.

I am often asked questions such as 'What's your favourite meal' or 'What's the best meal you've ever had'; people are invariably surprised by my answers. One of them would certainly be a succulent rump steak in Amsterdam, perfectly cooked and washed down with bottles of Freddy's finest, Heineken, which tasted great in its home city. I'm sure the dish, while undeniably spiffing, was made doubly palatable by the fact that I was glad to be alive following a mugging at knifepoint the night before – my second violent incident in Amsterdam in as many visits there.

Another would be a large plate of lentils eaten with gusto on a balmy evening in Cluny, at the southern tip of the Burgundy region. This meal, which consisted of nothing but the lentils – not even *petit sale* (a joint of bacon) – save maybe for some butter and parsley, is one of my all-time food highlights, because of the company, the setting – outside, at long trestle tables – and a few bottles of Brouilly de l'Année, label-less and slightly chilled. Unforgettable.

There are of course many more such 'favourite meals', often partnered with live music: one of them would certainly be having a civilised feed on a train. On the western and southern lines, you can sometimes get a decent steak, some goodish chips and the aforementioned bottle of Bordeaux. Consuming these is still, I am convinced, one of the best ways to watch Ireland hurtle by. And since the train is not likely to hurtle so much as trundle, there will always be time for the other half of that bottle – which will ensure that you arrive at your destination ready to face the rest of your day. You simply can't get the like on the TGV, which is probably a victim of its own speed: it now serves poor pizza, crummy *croques monsieurs* and wishy-washy wine.

Enough of this train-related banter! One of the first of the many Kildare castles I visited was Barberstown Castle, once owned by Eric Clapton, in the townland of Straffan. I was invited there once for a wedding supper, and a limo, no less, was duly dispatched to pick me up from the Green Room, now Shanahan's, on Stephen's Green in Dublin, where I was cheffing for a time. I remember leaving the front door that night, all very eighties-looking, in a black suit, and possibly shades (but I sincerely hope not). As usual, I had no fixed hairstyle, but at least I still had hair, and it wasn't grey.

As I stepped into the waiting limo, I therefore felt all at once very glamorous and not unlike a fool. At that precise moment, some Dublin gurrier outside spotted me and cried in thick Dublinese: 'Who de feck do you t'ink you are, you big eejit?' I don't think I stepped inside a limo again for twenty years.

Straffan of course is also home to the world-famous K Club and, further afield, Moyglare Manor – both establishments with attendant fine restaurants, even finer cellars – and helipads. Kildare is that sort of a county. We jaded, exhausted and impoverished restaurateurs used to decamp to Moyglare Manor on Sunday nights for a spot of pampering and luxury, as well as to give the elegant wine list a lash.

The chef of the K Club is Michel Flamme: could there be a better name for a chef? Michel rose to prominence in mid-eighties Dublin as the chef of the Mirabeau in Sandycove, when it was relaunched by Doreen and Eoin Clarke and was a grey-and-pink icon of fine dining.

Some of the most memorable meals I ever had in Ireland were in the Mirabeau: for that reason I am currently saving every cent to treat myself to one of his meals at the K Club. Twenty years has not dimmed the memory of some his finer signature dishes, such as medallions of lobster wrapped in lettuce – a revelation way back then. His saucing was perfect, his pasta better than anyone else's, his fish cookery peerless.

It was there, too, that I discovered what was to become my favourite wine. La Mouline, the flagship Côte Rotie from Guigal, was at that point in Ireland selling at £33 and £36 in Guilbaud's and the Mirabeau respectively. Best of all, no one had ever heard of it. I drank the lot. Later, a wine critic – Robert Parker, I believe – gave it a whopping hundred out of a hundred, and prices skyrocketed. I haven't been able to afford it for years.

Production was limited, and Ireland was only allowed something like twelve cases a year, then distributed in Ireland by Pat Smyth. I once managed to secure a case for my own restaurant for the bagatelle of £290. The very next day I got a call from a leading

London restaurant offering me £2,000 sterling for the same case. To sell would have been very naughty, eliciting a huge tut-tut, but I would never have done it anyway. It was more important to have the wine.

Less grand than the castles and helipads, but certainly not pedestrian, is the county town of Kildare. Naas was once the seat of the King of Leinster (the original Irish name is Nás na Ríogh, 'Meeting Place of the Kings') and is now the place to be in County Kildare. It is one of the fastest-growing towns in Europe, has no fewer than thirty pubs on its main street and offers an amazing variety of top-flight restaurants. The town oozes the confidence of modern Ireland.

First up is the superb Les Olives restaurant in the town centre, run by Olivier and Maeve Pauloin-Valory, a Mediterranean-style restaurant (as the name might indicate). This establishment is spoken of in hushed tones by some of my food-loving friends and boasts a fantastic wine list, as well as the kind of sexy, herby, tasty food that is reminiscent of purple-misted evenings in Provence. You should also try Lemongrass, one of our better Thai restaurants; it is part of an Irish chain, with outlets also in Maynooth and Galway.

But can there be any more impressive establishment than Osprey? This establishment has to be experienced at first hand. No description will suffice, except to say that it reminds me of hotels in Singapore which too were 'a world apart', as the hotel likes to style itself: all-encompassing, with multiple bars, a restaurant, and top-class facilities. This is one of the many contemporary hotels that have sprung up all over the country, offering what the marketing boffins like to term a 'different customer experience', such as Zuni in Kilkenny, 10 Sq in Belfast and the Morrison in Dublin (whose Halo restaurant gets a large thumbs-up from me).

Steak on a train? Perhaps I'll alight at Kildare more often.

This is the kind of main-course dish encountered all over Italy, and is simplicity itself. I used to enjoy it often in restaurants in Turin such as La Pace, in the company of friends, where the food was always utterly fresh and the swordfish could be enjoyed either as a carpaccio – in wafer-thin, raw slices – with fresh limes and Parmesan, or quickly grilled like this.

1 200g swordfish steak (or tuna or shark) per person
Juice of 1 lemon
Grated lemon zest
Olive oil
Oregano
Salt and black pepper

Heat the grill to high. Beat together the lemon juice, zest, olive oil and oregano. Pour this over the fish, making sure that it is coated on both sides, then season with salt and freshly ground black pepper.

Grill the fish according to taste: the Italians will cook it more than the French; swordfish should ideally be eaten quite rare. (It is ironic that Italians would either eat the fish completely raw as a carpaccio or, to my taste, overcook it when grilling.)

Serve immediately. An appropriate garnish would be a rocket salad.

DUBLIN

I didn't come to live in Dublin because I got a job on foot of a successful interview or because it was any part of a gastronomic master plan; not a bit of it. It was simply because that, within walking distance of my place of work, there was a food emporium selling groundnut or peanut oil from Lesieur of France and that clinched it for me. I'd been living in Wales for what seemed like an eternity (in my less kind moments I wish epicurean retribution upon Wales for its lack of decent eating places) – an eternity made worse by the fact that I'd lived in France for an in-between year, and now, back in Belfast, there was no peanut oil, no Dijon mustard, no spirit vinegar, in short no means of making vinaigrette. And that, friends, meant life wasn't worth living.

And so to Dublin in June 1979, for the simple reason that Dublin had all of those things. The emporium in question was McCambridges of Ranelagh (now in Galway); I think I increased its profits a thousand-fold in the years that I worked in Ranelagh while launching my career as 'The Man Who Eats Out Most in Ireland'. In those days, there wasn't much in Dublin save for a few scattered Italians around Dame Street, which I quickly discovered and feasted in regularly. Those were the days of La Taverna and Nicos, of which the latter still survives, serving unchanging, simple, dependable grub. It continues to be a great, old-fashioned spot for lunch; its sublime *fettuccine doppio burro* may be the sole reaons for my ample girth. It isn't the cheapest restaurant in town, given the rudimentary nature of its decor and service, but there are two reasons why it shall ever hold a place in my esteem: the unsung pianist who played 'Planxty Maguire' – a personal favourite of mine from O'Carolan's repertoire – for me every time I walked in, and the fact that they stock the regal Italian wines Solaia and Sassicaia at strangely low prices. (Oops, that's torn it.)

They were also the days of the Pancake HQ in Beresford Place, the Athena on Sundays in South Richmond Street – a Greek place which served tasteless Sunday roast lunches with the odd pseudo-ethnic departure like moussaka – and Captain America's, from which every budding foodie graduated. Dublin was far from a gourmet paradise in those days: nobody sat outside drinking weird coffee beverages, pesto was unheard of, and I can remember buying three-litre bottles of rough Italian quaffable wine for £1.59.

Somehow I began writing about traditional music as a sideline to my living (when not in restaurants, I could be found in bars playing my favourite reel, 'The Lads of Laois', on a battered banjo). Naturally enough, writing about music for *In Dublin* magazine led to me writing a second column, called 'Beano', about food – and, more specifically, restaurants – for them. I think I wrote for the magazine for about three years, fending off the popular myths that grew up alongside that I was saying 'I could do better' and that 'I would love to open a restaurant.'

Actually, nothing was further from my mind than opening my own place: I was doing very well, thank you, with my post-hippie lifestyle of music, food, drink – and most of my restaurant meals – paid for. It came as a shock when one day a chap rang me up and said: 'I hear you really want to open a restaurant.' The shock was even greater when I heard myself say 'Yes.' I duly went to inspect the premises and, without the slightest knowledge of economics, business, cooking or the daily grind of running a restaurant – and displaying an incredible and unenviable lack of sense – signed up, and opened up my own restaurant shortly thereafter.

The restaurant was named after the column. It was first mooted as 'Chez Beano' and then, with one of the characteristic turns of the diseased mind that is mine, I decided to deploy a dazzling bilingual pun, the secrets of which shall go with me to my grave (unless large sums of cash are proferred), and call it 'Shay Beano'. This establishment became a legend in other people's lunchtimes, caused me to die at least three times, moved premises, went up-, down- and side-market – and was the greatest craic ever. The day it opened, I stopped writing (and therefore stopped lambasting other establishments; tut tut, wouldn't have been fair) and stopped playing banjo and bouzouki, which I do regret. And just as I was getting good, too. But like Monty Python before me, the public decided that there was a Shay Beano and that I was he, and so, while I was forever Éamonn on the outside, I was always 'Shay' in the restaurant.

The stories from the Shay Beano years and the people I met there – and who stayed there until five o'clock in the morning (every night for ten years) – would of course fill another tome. Several stories stand out, however. There was of course the opening weeks of the restaurant, when I quickly found out that I didn't have a notion of what I was doing and had to learn in less than a month what Escoffier had been banging on about. A 'feature' of the restaurant was that Saturday night was couscous night. Yes, it may well have been twenty years ahead of its time: I still hear the voices going 'Ya big eejit, Éamonn.'

It had never occurred to me that, unlike my legendary dinner parties, where people who ought to have known better had positively encouraged me to 'do this professionally', customers had every right to arrive at a time of their choosing within opening hours. This was the scene on our fourth Saturday when three customers walked in and ordered different couscouses from the menu. Trouble was, they no longer existed, as the meats in question had long since been boiled to bits in the vegetable broth they were meant to simmer in. It had never occurred to me to, well, turn the heat down. But them's the benefits of a third-level education, folks. The emaciated customers quite rightly confronted me with the stinging sentence: 'And you're the so-called restaurant writer who had the gall to criticise others.' Harrumph. Trouble was, worse was to come when I realised that I'd also forgotten to order any coffee or, indeed, stock up on wine. That night, I felt like closing the restaurant after just four weeks, but of course, *la nuit porte conseil,* and by Monday, after a weekend of forcing myself to listen to Slim Dusty's 'A Pub with No Beer', I had made up my mind to 'get my act together.' Thenceforth, awful nights like that never reoccurred.

The other famous incident concerning the restaurant was the night I appeared on Mike Murphy's radio programme for live banter with Sean Kinsella of Mirabeau, then the restaurant that was spoken of in hushed tones in Dublin-society circles, where prices didn't figure on the menus and bills were always a surprise. I had originally refused to appear on the show, as the fact that I did all my cooking by myself in my flat (yes, this was completely illegal) and ferried it down in a fleet of taxis every night (now you know why Dublin taxis always smelt of couscous, *harissa* and *ras-al-hanout* (a typical North African spice mix) for several years in the mid-eighties) meant that I had little time to be swanning around in radio studios or doing live interviews by phone on talk-in shows. Nevertheless, just after 5 PM, the researcher rang me on an old black communal A-B phone in the hall and simply whispered: 'You're on.' Oh, we had a right to-do on the steam radio, and it was classic radio, but I didn't give it a second thought until the taxi brought me down Kildare Street and I saw the queue from the Alliance Française to the front of my signless and phoneless restaurant and realised just who had won the debate. Mind you, the driver had been regaling me with tales of 'De fellah on de radio earlier, jaze it was grea'.' Big deal, I thought: I had only eight tables, and they were all booked for about five weeks solid. We proceeded to turn four-fifths of the people away, including, to my eternal shame, my own mother. Turning people away was to become a damaging feature of the restaurant.

There were other rumours about the restaurant, including the classic 'He doesn't put salt and pepper on his tables.' This was not strictly true: we put the salt and pepper cellars to one side, available on request, for the simple reason that people kept half-inching ('robbing', in Dublinese) my lovely Villeroy and Boch sets. Mind you, the sight of diners automatically covering their 'dinner' in salt before they actually tasted it was a feature of eighties gastronomy and a sight I never got used to. Oh, and the twin expressions 'It's a good complaint' delivered by all and sundry when you announced for example that you were 'busy these days' – or 'It's delicious' when a plate of food was put down in front of them. 'It looks delicious, you mean, you haven't tasted it yet' I would mentally hiss ten times a night for ten long years, consoling myself with the knowledge that 'When oi write me buke' I'd get my own back. Tee-hee.

I certainly felt an animosity towards the concept of having potatoes – awful Irish 'balls of flour' potatoes – with every meal, and I was forever at loggerheads with customers about the absence of same where I deemed it inappropriate. This never went down too well, the customer expecting potato and I pointing out that they were eating the tubers on the other 364 days of the year. One night, instead of receiving compliments about an otherwise perfectly executed meal, I got only complaints about the potatoless fare. To my shame, I let fly at the customer; bad words were included, for which I am humbly contrite. Only in Ireland could potatoes work up such passions.

These days in Dublin, restaurateurs and chefs can serve up what they like, and the twenty-somethings will happily chomp on dishes *sans* potatoes. The busy city and suburbs full of restaurants of every shade could not have been imagined in the eighties, when we estimated that there were six thousand diners all going round in a circle and little passing trade from other countries. It's a terrific city to eat out in, and if the prices are still, uh, *somewhat* higher than those of mainland Europe, then the signs are that, with the advent of the euro, a democratization in relation to prices is happening, with many establishments becoming more affordable. I have long had a golden rule when eating out in Dublin to eat in the best establishments at lunchtime, for a bargain was always to be found then, and in the cheaper establishments at night.

These days even that rule has been knocked on its head, with excellent and cheap meals to be had in wonderful, atmospheric places such as Ar Vicoletto on Crowe Street and the Old Mill in the heart of Temple Bar. Those two restaurants are currently top of my list for both lunch and dinner because, apart from their honest pricing, they are authentic. In Ar Vicoletto, for instance, you feel as though you have stepped into a trattoria in some back street in Rome, and the cuisine is spot-on.

I have to confess that I'm tired of 'trying' places, and tired of overpriced restaurants. If a place is good, I will go back and have the same dish over and over again – if that too was good. And this is how it is in 'Ar Vic', as I have affectionately dubbed it. The lunchtime bargain of two courses with a glass of wine and the best espresso in town for   12 speaks for itself. The staff are sharp, courteous and attentive, and the food is very good: generous, toothsome and cooked without flourish but with understanding. Don't miss the spaghetti carbonara at lunchtime – the first time I have had an authentic representation of this dish in Dublin – or their *bruschette varie,* which are almost a meal in themselves.

The crowning glory is from the à la carte menu: *saltimbocca alla Romana.* This, too, is a perfectly judged dish: thin strips of tasty veal with a strip of salty, smoky, piquant Parma ham, the whole brought to life in mid-flight by the perfect placing of a fresh sage leaf – the 'jump-in-the-mouth' of the dish's name – offset by a simple light butter sauce. Ar Vicoletto is one of Dublin's jewels: a small neighbourhood restaurant that does its job superbly and never fails to please.

Lahcen Iouani's 'Old Mill' has been through many name changes but remains a true French restaurant of the old school – and a pleasure to return to, as the food is both timeless and charming. The descriptions on the menu do not convey the excellence or robustness of the cooking here: it always comes as an agreeable surprise to be genuinely taken aback by confident and satisfying cooking. The menu rarely changes: such staples as black sole on the bone, guinea fowl with blue-cheese sauce, and roast poussin with tarragon jus are perfect examples of restaurant cooking done properly.

Lahcen is Moroccan, and from time to time specialities from his country appear on the specials board. A little-known fact about the place is that, if you have a word with him and give forty-eight hours' notice, he will cook a full Moroccan meal for four or more – a mighty and succulent feed.

The reader might be surprised by the absence from these pages of some of the loftier, starred names around town. Although some of these places have fallen into extreme disfavour with me, I still like the *grands établissements:* it's just that I choose others besides the obvious. For instance, the Tea Room in U2's Clarence Hotel, which has been my favourite for a long time now. The earthiness, nay rock and roll, ethos of many of the dishes (like John Dory with deep-fried snails or the smashing 'study in bacon and cabbage') appeals to me. Their offerings somehow seem more real than a number of the ethereal offerings in the Well-known Places, where sometimes you don't know whether to eat the food or take a photograph of it, and where the table settings should include a magnifying glass beside the knives and forks to help you find the food.

A recent visit to Les Frères Jacques revealed that restaurant to be as kicking as ever, quietly getting on with the business of top-class food without fuss or star-hunting. It does it as it ever did: the fresh fish presented raw to you before ordering, elegant saucing that you can enjoy, not send out an explorer to find, and various *amuse-gueules* and titbits to complete the luxury of the occasion. This to me is what other so-called French restaurants should be: French, serving French food with panache. But so many have lost their way in their reach for the stars and their embracing of a pan-European approach, which has resulted in a loss of identity and flavour as national subtleties are ignored and discouraged.

Of particular interest on the Dublin food scene is the growth of the wine bar. This development is thanks to the daddy of them all, the basement wine bar known as La Cave. It is difficult for me to have to admit that it has been around since 1987 – and that I was in there from the beginning. La Cave is unique: a tiny, cramped place, a wine-lovers' home from home, serving great food. It can be somewhere to have an espresso at eleven thirty, a lunchtime spot serving great bistro food – with sometimes a hankering to the grand until mid-afternoon – then, a place for coffee or indelicate wine drinking, listening to Piaf and Brel. Finally, it is a place for an aperitif at around six and dinner from seven, after which it turns into a great African nightclub, serving up soukous, samba and salsa until the wee small hours.

Now, of course, it has many imitators and rivals – a trend which is very welcome. Try Havana just off Camden Street for almost exclusively Hispanic music and food: another excellent nightspot. Ely on Ely Place has an enviable wine list, with dozens by the glass, and is also one of the few to offer Roederer by the glass, for which it gets a large thumbs-up!

The latest addition to the scene is Peploe's on Stephen's Green, run by Barry Canny, late of Browne's Brasserie. Here too is a convivial bar area, with many elegant wines by the very elegant glass, and very well executed comfort food to match, as evidenced by a recent shepherd's pie I had there: the thinking man's alernative to Neurofen when nursing a hangover. Two glasses of Bordeaux or whatever the informed bar staff recommend and you're as right as rain.

Every time my train pulls into Connolly Station I'm already thinking about where I'll eat. Will it be French Paradox for the foie gras platter? Pearl Brasserie for the foie gras with rhubarb and strawberries? Steps of Rome for meatballs? Casbah on Crowe Street for couscous, tagine and *zaalouk*? Chips in Ocean with a bottle of Becks? The girls in Baccaro – and don't mind the food? Or Lahcen's fantastic omelettes that banish hangovers?

*

I'm very proud of the people who worked with me in Shay Beano over the years. People like Christophe Favaudon, who subsequently worked in Guilbaud's, the Mirabeau and Fitzers, and a person for whom the word 'indefatigable' was coined. These days Christophe's unfailingly cheery countenance is to be found in his eponymous outlet in the Epicurean Food Hall off Liffey Street, where he is still feeding legions of Dubliners and scoring high points with his 'roast in a roll' lunches, which were named as being one of the top tastes in Dublin in a recent edition of the *Dubliner* magazine. He has now added a second restaurant, with partner Joe, behind Chief O'Neill's in Smithfield.

There was Philippe too, a giant of a man, slightly chubby and twenty-three going on ninety. His poise and effortless movement between the narrow tables made all the girls swoon. (His elegant but old-fashioned clobber made him look much older than his years, but there's no accounting for women.) He was a wonderful maître d'hôtel and I was privileged to have him in my employ: I only secured his services because Patrick Guilbaud didn't turn up on time for his interview. When the girls weren't after him, every other restaurateur in Dublin was. Last I heard, he was chief steward on the *Orient Express*.

What would I have done without Raoul Rodriguez? It was Raoul who oversaw the restaurant's transition from imitation *routier* in South Leinster Street to smart restaurant in Stephens Street. He also taught me all that I never knew about cooking in a kitchen. I foolishly introduced him to Mary Pat, who was to become his wife, and the pair duly set off on some hare-brained scheme to open a restaurant in the British West Indies after paddling there from Argentina, or suchlike.

They're still there. The restaurant, today called Hibernia, is one of the most successful restaurants in Anguilla, and is a perennial favourite of some of the most well-heeled celebrities in the world. Raoul has won umpteen awards, and, repesenting Anguilla, came second in the whole of the Caribbean in awards organised by the Caribbean Culinary Federation. The pair fly to Thailand during their low season. Raoul finds recipes there and adapts them to local West Indian produce: he has effectively developed a unique cuisine by marrying Thai techniques with West Indian tradition and French know-how. You can find out more about their remarkable restaurant at *www.hiberniarestaurant.com*. The other day he was kind enough to create this recipe for this book. We hope you enjoy it.

MEDAILLON DE LANGOUSTE CROUSTILLANTE
VELOUTÉ DE POTIRON À LA CITRONNELLE

for the velouté (a smooth, creamy soup):
One and a half pounds of pumpkin, diced
2 lemongrass stalks, finely chopped
200ml coconut milk
2 scallions, finely chopped
500ml chicken stock

for the lobster:
2 lobster tails
4 lemongrass stalks
Pinch chilli flakes (optional)

for the batter:
1 egg
2 tablespoons flour
50g crushed-glass noodles

Serves 4

for the velouté:
Heat the coconut milk in a pan, then add the lemongrass and
pumpkin. Let it simmer for five minutes, then add the chicken
stock. Bring to the boil, reduce the heat and simmer until the
pumpkin is soft. Liquidize and strain. Season with salt and pepper.

for the lobster:
Slice the lobster tails lengthways to give four halves. Dip them in
the egg, roll them in the flour, and then in the noodles. (Don't do
this in advance, as they will go soggy.) Use the lemon-grass stalks
to make brochettes. Deep-fry the brochettes at 180°C.

to serve:
Pour some velouté in a soup bowl and place the lobster on top.
Sprinkle on the chilli flakes, if using.

There was a fashion in the 1980s for cooking shark, the popularity of which seems to have waned in favour of swordfish and tuna. I think I still prefer shark, though its shelf life is much shorter than those other two fish and it must be binned if not fresh. I ate it in the West Indies, first as 'shark 'n' bake' on Maracas beach in Trinidad – glorious beer-and-sunshine fare you want to treat all your mates to, Jamie Oliver-style – and subsequently in Gosier, Guadeloupe, as a subtle *blanquette de requin*, which was a brilliant marriage of a French classic with local produce.

Back in Ireland, I cooked it a lot in the Shay Beano days, and if I may be permitted a little name-dropping (in this otherwise-devoid-of-name-dropping tome!), barbecued it *en brochette* for Mark Knopfler at a private party for Dire Straits in Dublin. Mr Knopfler, the ultimate gentleman, rewarded me, as he had promised, with a bottle of his on-tour Nuits St Georges, dispatched from the Westbury Hotel the very next day. Bono and chums, too, used to order it by phone to Windmill Lane Studios while they were recording *The Unforgettable Fire* (fnarr, fnarr) – the only Shay Beano takeaway that we ever did. (If I'd had more commercial sense, I could have been rich.)

I cannot for the life of me remember what sauces we used to partner shark with: those brain cells are long since dead. But for a while, I was involved with another restaurant, La Fiesta in Camden Street, which was great fun. I had a dish of brochette of shark there with Puy lentils. (It was my lentil period.) Anyway, one day I asked an aspiring new French employee to cook the dish for me, and he did – better than I ever could. Unfortunately, once he got the job, he never again put quite the same effort into cooking, and I had to let him go, with expletives aforethought. Still, he left me the one great missing ingredient for my shark-and-lentil dish: oranges.

500g fresh shark loin, cubed
Zest and juice of 1 lime
1 clove garlic, crushed
Olive oil
Sea salt
Crushed black pepper
Zest and juice of 2 oranges
Balsamic vinegar
200g Puy lentils
Chopped parsley and coriander
2 shallots, peeled

First, soak the lentils in tepid water while preparing the shark. In a bowl, combine the shark with a little olive oil to coat, the lime zest and juice, garlic, salt and pepper, and leave to one side to marinate. (These days, I'd probably replace the salt with a few drops of *nam pla,* the ubiquitous Thai fish sauce.)

Place the Puy lentils in a saucepan full of water and bring to the boil. Keep one eye on them and check regularly until they are cooked just so (anything from half an hour to an hour, depending on how long they were soaked for) – that is, with a slight resistance to the bite. Drain.

Skewer the cubes of shark. (If using wooden skewers, dip them in cold water first to prevent burning.) I wouldn't put any vegetables between each cube of shark: it's far too much trouble, and the veg will only detract from the great taste of the shark. Place on a grill pan or below the grill in the oven. Remember that the lime juice will have part-cooked the flesh. so turn rapidly and do not leave to cook for too long.

Place the lentils in a pan on a low heat with a little water. Add the orange zest and juice, salt and pepper to taste, and a splash of balsamic vinegar. Stir in some of the parsley and coriander leaf. Finally, grate the shallots into the lentil mixture and stir until thoroughly warmed through.

Spoon the lentils onto a warm plate, place one or two brochettes of shark on top and garnish with the remaining parsley and coriander. If you have any more limes, you could put a wedge on the side. And if you have any Angostura Bitters, a couple of drops on top will impart that true Caribbean flavour.

Stick on the latest by Krosfyah from Barbados, walk to your table, pour a really cool one, add a dash of Encora's Hot Pepper Sauce – if you're able for it – to the side of the plate and devour.

I used to love making this classic dish in the restaurant. It was for two people, was roasted on the bone, used to have marrow jelly in the sauce, and was served rare – come to think of it, for all these reasons it's probably banned today. I recently asked for a blue steak in an Irish restaurant and was asked to sign a piece of paper acknowledging my culpability in the event of my subsequent death. Have we gone mad?

Côte de boeuf is a French cut that any good butcher will do for you: ask for a French rib of beef on the bone. The sauce is very simple, but very effective. There is no particular reason for choosing Beaujolais as the red wine for this sauce, but it seems to work, maybe because it's light and fruity, always in party mode, and has the right balance for the heavier meat. Suffice to say that the Dublin wine merchant Richard Verling, who often ordered this dish, used to say that if he could bottle this sauce, he'd make a fortune.

This is a dish that separates the Irish into two camps, however: those who enjoy rare meat that you take pleasure in chewing and savouring the juices from, and those who won't touch anything but a fillet that contains no fat, presents little challenge to the choppers, and disappears down the throat without much manifesting its presence. If you are of the former camp, then this dish and cut is for you. It should be cooked no more than medium, otherwise it will be tough and uninteresting.

One *côte de boeuf* is sufficient for two people; simply get more if you are catering for a larger party. Odd numbers are obviously a nuisance: the cut is generally served to two people in a restaurant. Then again, I once witnessed some Russian sailors in a restaurant in Lyon wolf two *côtes de boeuf* each: the waitress was frightened. The quantities given below are not for submariners!

1 rib of beef on the bone (enough for two)
6 cloves of garlic: 5 cut into slivers, 1 crushed
1 bottle of Beaujolais
Large bunch of parsley
Salt and black pepper
2 shallots, finely chopped
Red-wine vinegar
Beef stock
6 new potatoes per person
Olive oil and Irish butter

Oil the meat, then insert the garlic into the flesh, using the point of a knife. Salt and pepper both sides. Heat a pan with a small amount of butter and oil and add the meat, turning several times to brown on both sides. Then place the pan (if it is all-metal, otherwise transfer to an oven dish) in an oven preheated to 200°C. Cooked rare will take about twenty minutes; allow a further five to ten minutes for medium.

I like to serve this dish with roast potatoes only. I generally parboil them, then add them to the pan containing the meat just before placing it in the oven. This finishes their cooking and gives a nice crisp edge to the skins. I usually don't partner it with any other vegetable, believing the meat, the sauce and the tubers to be sufficient, but if you wish you could serve with a little spinach, green beans or wild mushrooms.

After twenty minutes (or a little more for medium-done), remove the pan from the oven, place the meat to one side, and return the pan to a high flame on your cooker, adding a little butter and the chopped shallots. When the oil begins to smoke, add a generous glass of wine to combine with the pan juices. Add a tablespoonful of red-wine vinegar at this point. Crush the remaining cloves of garlic and add them, together with copious amounts of roughly chopped parsley, to the pan. Add the beef stock and another glass of wine and leave to simmer.

To carve: with a sharp knife, remove the large chunk of meat from the bone by cutting along the back of the bone. When it has come away from the bone in one piece, throw that into the sauce and then carve the meat into thick slices. (In the old days, the serving of a *côte de boeuf* involved the meat being carved and served to the couple, with the man getting the rib-bone on his plate. In these less sexist days, I remove the bone before carving and throw it too into the sauce.) Arrange the slices fan-like on two warmed plates, and place the potatoes around it.

Finish off the sauce by reducing it until thickened and then adding some chilled knobs of butter for an elegant sheen. Add a little more wine to loosen the sauce if necessary, then strain it into a sauce-boat, leaving the garlic, parsley, shallots and bone behind, obtaining only the heady, brown-red sauce. Pour the sauce around the meat and potatoes, sprinkle with parsley, and serve.

I have noticed that, in our quest to plunder the world's cuisines, we are being presented with new bottled sauces next to the 'Provençal' couscous, Thai this and that, and northeast Tuscan 'rub' for fish. This time it's the turn of South Africa and the curry sauces of Cape Malay.

I have been hearing a lot about this cuisine from pals who used to live there. These sauces turn out to be a very pleasant surprise. If the bottled stuff is this good, it must surely be better when you make it yourself.

Over the years, the Fitzers chain in Dublin has been responsible for introducing new and exotic flavours to Irish palates: their newest outlet, the Chatham Brasserie in Chatham Street, just off Grafton Street, is typical of their restaurants: fun, no-nonsense eating offering great value.

The chef at the Chatham, Jaco, is from South Africa. One of the most popular items on their menu is his Cape Malay curry, which, after a sucessful bout of arm-wrestling, he has kindly given me the recipe for.

25g each of the following:
Cumin seeds
Fennel seeds
Star anise
Green cardamom seeds
Juniper berries
Coriander seeds

4 chicken fillets, cubed
Turmeric
Bay leaves
Garam masala
Flour
2 onions, finely sliced

3 cloves of garlic, crushed
Fresh ginger, grated
1 tin of chopped tomatoes

for the spice mix:
Grind the spices to a coarse powder in a food blender.

to make the curry:
Coat the chicken in a mixture of the flour and garam masala. Heat some peanut oil in a pot, place the chicken in this and leave for a few minutes with the lid on, turning occasionally.

Once the outside has become golden-brown, add enough of the ground-spice mix to coat the chicken. Then add the sliced onions, ginger and garlic.

Leave to cook for a minute before adding the chopped tomatoes, which should cover the chicken. Add a little water if necessary to cover: it will evaporate during cooking.

Cook for about thirty minutes over a low heat. Make sure to stir frequently: the flour will thicken the sauce but will also burn if left to catch on the bottom of the pot.

Serve with rice.

WICKLOW

You know of course that Wicklow is referred to as the 'Garden of Ireland' and that this is as much to do with the county's scenery as with the inhabitants' penchant for growing organic produce, for which it is rightly famous. Wicklow's countryside is simply beautiful: lushly green, with rolling hillsides and, no doubt, endless golf courses – which we'll ignore now as my eyes begin to glaze over.

Like Wexford, it boasts many fine places to stay and eat, but it is particularly famous for its grand country homes, all within easy reach of Dublin. Try the magnificent Tinakilly House or the lovely Hunters of Rathnew, ideal for a Saturday night away or a Sunday lunch. The county is full of beautiful places to go, such as Glendalough, magnificent gardens like Powerscourt or Mount Usher, and tidy little towns such as Avoca (now, unfortunately, better known as the setting for *Ballykissangel)* and Arklow (made famous by Van Morrison with the track 'Streets of Arklow', on his 1974 album *Veedon Fleece)*.

I can always see the beautiful azure Wicklow Mountains in the distance as the train rolls into Connolly Station from Belfast. Each and every time, the hills remind me of happy Sunday evenings spent in Wicklow, when, week after week, I'd head out by taxi or DART to the Cypriot restaurant the Tree of Idleness, on the seafront at Bray. The Tree was run by Akis and Susan Courtellas, who set up there after losing their original restaurant in Cyprus in 1974 following the Turkish invasion. Sadly, the restaurant is no more, and Akis himself passed away in 1991.

But I shall forever associate Wicklow with the many nights of food and laughter I spent there: a casual ouzo in the cool entrance, peopled with backgammon-playing expats chattering away in Greek, before proceeding to table for my early introduction to the delights of hummus and pitta, *yemista,* moussaka, *kleftico* (a recipe for which is given on page 37), *dolmades* and umpteen *mezze* shared with friends. And the wine list? Ah, who could forget it? I must have worked my way through it: fantastic Bordeaux at minimal prices, rare and odd vintages, the chance to taste a '72 Latour for £32 Irish. Nineteen seventy-two was a dreadful year for Bordeaux, but Latour is Latour. At that price, it was worth taking the risk.

I remember the night Bono was there with his family, celebrating the single 'Desire' going to No. 1 in the UK charts. He wanted more wine but did not wish to seem extravagant in front of his parents. He spotted my delighted face as I supped on the Latour and asked Akis what I was drinking. When told of its pedigree and price, he immediately ordered a bottle. We've had a nodding, conspiratorial acquaintance ever since.

Never one to rest on his Tree of Idleness, Akis was forever adding new dishes to the menu and was probably in the forefront, way back then, of today's practice of marrying local ingredients to a foreign cuisine. I distinctly remember his stuffed Wicklow lamb with feta and blackcurrant vinegar: now *there* was a dish. My version of it is given below.

The many diners who ate there will also remember the heaving dessert trolley at the end. Yes, there were quite a few heaving desserts on it, but for the most part it was stocked with all manner of exotic fruits, many of them in wine or Commandaria port (beloved of Richard the Lionheart and mentioned in the Bible), most of them as yet unheard of by most Irish people. Today they're commonplace, but it was thanks to Akis and his daring cuisine that a whole generation, myself included, learned so much about the foodstuffs that existed far beyond the garden of Ireland.

I remember very well Akis introducing flavours like this in his restaurant. It was probably in the Tree of Idleness that I encountered fruit vinegars for the first time (apart from the ubiquitous raspberry vinegar which I was partnering – rather more prosaically, though believing myself to be hip – with pork chops and the *salade folle,* or warm salad, that was de rigueur in the eighties.

Lamb responds very well to blackcurrant vinegar, which has remained in vogue, as it was never subjected to the over-exposure from which raspberry vinegar suffered. I have been known to add a splash of blackcurrant vinegar to Irish stew (which, when I cooked it in New York, was greeted with much hearty back-slapping and cries of 'Dude, your *stoo,* it's like, uh, *awesome!*': lads, it's just a splash of blackcurrant vinegar), as well as to *kleftico,* which, in the words of the old Jameson advertisement, is 'shocking but nice'.

Here is a version inspired by Akis's dish. He would not have served pulses with his version: if you don't fancy the beans, by all means replace them with potatoes, which you could roast in the oven along with the lamb.

1 leg of lamb
1 block of feta cheese, cubed
Splash of blackcurrant vinegar
300g haricot beans, soaked overnight in warm water
5 medium-sized onions, left whole and with the skins on
Glass of white wine
1 bag of fresh spinach leaves
Fresh mint leaves
4 cloves of garlic, 2 cut into thin slivers
Bay leaves
Salt and pepper, and a little butter

Using a small knife, insert the slivers of garlic into the flesh of the lamb. Heat an all-metal pan on a medium heat. Add olive oil and a knob of butter, then place the lamb on the pan and lightly brown it all over. Put the pan in an oven preheated to 190°C and leave to roast for forty-five minutes for pink, longer for well-done.

Put the haricot beans in a pot of salted water with a few bay leaves, bring to the boil, reduce the heat and leave to simmer. Add the onions to the pot for about ten minutes, then remove. Blanch the spinach for a few seconds in boiling, salted water, drain, refresh under cold running water and reserve.

Break up the cubed feta further with a fork or a wooden spoon. Make an emulsion with the blackcurrant vinegar and salt and pepper by whisking these ingredients together with a fork. Julienne the mint and place to one side.

Cut the part-cooked onions in half, lengthways, skin-on, and rub all over with olive oil before placing, flesh-side down, in either a hot grill pan or a frying pan. This will mark the onions, to create an attractive, edible garnish. (I hate putting things on a plate that can't be eaten!)

When the lamb is cooked, remove it from the pan and place to one side: it will carve more easily after it has cooled slightly. Return the pan to the hob, turn the heat up and deglaze the pan with a glass of white wine and a further splash of the vinegar. Strain into a saucepan. Return to the heat with another glass of wine, and leave on a low heat to reduce. When ready to serve, add the feta and vinegar mixture, and a small cube or two of butter to give a sheen to the sauce, and adjust the seasoning.

Add the spinach to the pan and return the pan briefly to the oven (with the heat off): this will warm up the spinach without cooking it further – and save on the washing up! Drain the beans, return them to the pot, and add a generous knob of butter and salt and pepper. Carve the lamb, place on a plate with a generous spoonful of the beans. Place a helping of spinach on the other side of the plate. Spoon the sauce around the lamb, then sprinkle the chopped mint over the ensemble.

TAGINE D'AGNEAU AUX ABRICOTS
– LAMB TAGINE WITH APRICOTS

The cuisine of the Maghreb, and of Morocco in particular, is one of the world's greatest and is named by no less an authority than Robert Carrier as second only to the cuisines of France and China.

Stories and anecdotes abound about Moroccan cooking, from the national dish – couscous – to the use of rancid butter *(s'men)*, the jars of preserved lemons, the incorporation of hashish in sweet cakes, the marvellous combination of spices that is *ras-al-hanout,* the delicate *briks* (a pastry envelope made with the impossibly thin *warka* pastry and usually containing a runny egg and tuna), the sheer magic of a *méchoui* (spit-roasted lamb).

Tagines (the name comes from the earthenware casserole with a conical lid in which the dish is simmered) are simply aromatic stews. Were spices such as *ras-al-hanout* not used, the food would be little more than boiled or roasted meats.

Tagines are often served with rice, but in this instance the dish should be served with grain couscous, to demonstrate the wonderful, delicate, aromatic flavour that comes from this most bland of grains.

200g dried apricots, soaked in warm water overnight
5cm length of ginger, peeled and julienned
450g red onions, peeled and sliced
2 red chillies, deseeded and finely chopped
Flat-leaf parsley, finely chopped
Coriander leaves, finely chopped
Cumin seeds
1.5kg (3lb) neck fillet of lamb, butterflied and cut into cubes
Olive oil
Paprika
Cinnamon stick
Chicken stock
300ml plain yogurt
Salt and pepper

for the couscous:
300g couscous
Ground cinnamon (optional)
Butter
Raisins (optional)
Glass of salted water

Toast the cumin seeds under a grill for around half a minute (make sure they do not burn), then grind them to a powder. Oil the lamb and season it with salt and pepper.

Mark the lamb on both sides by flashing on a very hot grill pan. Put to one side. Fry the onions in the oil until transparent, then stir in the chillies, paprika and cumin. After two more minutes of frying, add the lamb, apricots and cinnamon stick. Then add the stock and bring the entire mixture to the boil. Leave to simmer over a reduced heat until the lamb is tender.

Before serving, remove the cinnamon stick. Stir in the yoghurt, parsley and coriander.

for the couscous:
For best results, couscous should be cooked over steam in a special pan called a *couscousier*. An acceptable result can also be achieved as follows: cook it in a frying pan in a little water, then leave in the pan in a hot oven for a few minutes until the couscous is fluffy and all the grains are separate. If any grains are still sticking together, roll the couscous between the palms of your hands to separate them. (You will need a bowl of cold water to dip your hands into in order to counteract the heat of the couscous!) Finally, mix the couscous with a generous knob of butter, and a pinch of cinnamon and raisins if desired.

CARLOW

There was a time when there were a great many things that bothered me about Ireland. We drank tea, but the tea commonly found in the shops was poor. We ate shedloads of potatoes, but they were fit for little other than mash: they fell apart when cooking and tasted of nothing in particular. Lastly, we love beer but, with the exception of one famous black drink with a creamy-white head, our beers were insipid and full of chemicals.

For a long time it seemed as though nothing would ever change; then, the 'Irish food revolution' ushered in a whole new way of thinking about our eating habits, our lifestyles and our food products in general. Suddenly, in tandem with this new food culture, a wealth of micro-breweries established themselves, notably the Porterhouse in Dublin's Parliament Street, where one could not only watch the brews being made but also sample the result in a convivial setting. Follow me now, up to Carlow.

Carlow is one of Ireland's smallest counties and one which, suprisingly, I have visited a great deal more than many others, despite the fact that it is not noted as one of Ireland's foodie regions. In the bad old days, Carlow was not particularly well served by public transport: I remember only too well, having just missed one of the only two daily trains to Dublin, spending the next six hours standing in the pouring rain just outside the station, trying to hitch a lift. Eventually I gave up and ambled onto the later train, a shivering wreck.

If that had happened today, I could have spent many a happy hour in the Carlow Brewing Company, just beside the station. The brewery, a small, pristine operation housed in a beautiful old stone building, was established by the O'Hara brothers, Seamus and Eamonn, in 1998. It is a joy to visit and a delightful place to sit and sample the wares.

Brewing in Carlow and county is not without precedent. In the past, many brewing companies had been established in this area of the Barrow Valley, long famous for the production of hops and malt. The nineteenth century saw at least five breweries operating in County Carlow, but these had all closed by the end of that century.

The Carlow Brewing Company's product range includes a stout, a pale ale and a classic lager. Astonishingly, the O'Hara brothers have already established themselves on the international beer scene. O Hara's Stout, for example, recently took the Gold Medal for the world's best stout at the Millennium Brewing Industry International Awards, ahead of seventy-four other stouts and porters.

Of particular interest is the Curim Gold Celtic Wheat Beer, a revival of a traditional Irish beer brewed in the area by the early Celtic inhabitants. (The name 'Curim' comes from the Irish 'coirm' – cognate with modern Welsh 'cwrw', meaning 'ale'.) It is the kind of beer which was mentioned in the saga *Táin Bó Cuailgne* and which King Conor Mac Nessa spent one third of the day drinking. (This was the one thing in my lectures on Old Irish that caught my attention: the fact that King Conor also spent a third of the day playing chess and watching boys play hurley put me to sleep, as did past subjunctives and neuter nouns.)

I have long been a champion of a cool beer as an aperitif, and the Curim Gold Celtic Wheat Beer is the kind of crisp beer that is an ideal partner for food – though its thrist-quenching capacities are not in dispute. Some dishes should ideally be accompanied with beer rather than wine: the obvious ones are barbecues, hot dogs, burgers and the like, but dishes involving eggs – omelette, *tortine,* quiche Lorraine and Alsace onion tart (a recipe for which is given on page 171) – are also excellent with beer. Remember too that a crisp salad served with these dishes will also respond well to beer, since it is never recommended to serve wine with a vinaigrette *'Car le vin n'aime pas son petit frère, le vinaigre.'*

Classic Irish food suits beer: heart-warming bacon and buttery cabbage would be admirably partnered by Curim, a half-dozen oysters in the shell with a bottle of O'Hara's Stout would be excellent, as would the same drink with a piping-hot bowl of well-made Irish stew – bearing in mind the old French adage of 'a bottle on the table and a bottle in the dish'.

These beers would also adapt themselves for use in the actual cooking of new Irish food: mussels could be steamed with Curim instead of white wine, for example, while the stout could be used to add a twist to the Belgian classic of *carbonnade* with Irish beef (brief stewed in beer). I am delighted to offer a few such recipes below.

It is difficult to envisage a time when Ireland might produce its own wine (though a couple of small attempts are being made, producing Germanic-style white wines, near Cork) – unless dramatic changes happen to the climate. It is encouraging in the meantime to see breweries like the Carlow Brewing Company not just come into existence but also succeed.

Finally, I can think of no finer place to sample these wonderful Irish beers – apart from in the brewery itself – than in the magnificent setting of the famous Carlow pub and restaurant the Lord Bagenal in Leighlinbridge, beside the River Barrow. The menu is daring, revelling in the tastes of traditional Ireland but offering a modern take on them. For instance, the restaurant offers 'crubeens', or pigs' trotters, served with sweetbreads, glazed with Irish honey and stuffed with truffles!

You've a dinner party coming up and you want to serve them something original as an aperitif – not the usual gin and tonics, vodka Martinis and, in these post-Celtic Tiger climes, glasses of champagne, God between us and all harm. Well, here's the very thing: it can be made up in advance, even weeks ahead. In fact, the longer you keep it, the better it gets. Serve it as an aperitif or as a wine to accompany dessert, or just drink it on a warm summer's afternoon while listening to 'She Moves On' from Paul Simon's *Rhythm of the Saints* or the very rare 'Guantanamera' by Youssou N'Dour and the Super Étoile de Dakar. This drink is related to the classic aperitif from Armagnac the Pousse-Rapière, which is made with sparkling wine.

The recipe comes from the Landes district of France. A wine from there would be ideal; in Ireland, try a white Marsanne, a Petit Chablis or an Italian Pinot Grigio.

    1 litre white wine
    Zest of three oranges and one lemon
    A pinch of cinammon
    3 cloves
    125g sugar
    Two measures of Armagnac

Put all the ingredients in a hermetically sealed jar (multiply the quantities if desired) and then place in the fridge. After two weeks, strain, pour into old white-wine bottles, and keep cool.

KILKENNY

The first thing you must do on arrival in Kilkenny city is head for the Marble City Bar, have a drink and contemplate what you're going to do with yourself. It's a great bar, the colour scheme is *über*-cool, and while you're there you can have a pint of the local brew, Smithwicks, from the oldest brewery in the land. No doubt there's all sorts of marketing nonsense invented about this ale's provenance concerning some twelfth-century monks who used to brew their own nearby, but sure what harm? Didn't the French swallow all that old guff we told them about George Killian's non-existent Kilkenny brew?

I have to admit that I'm not too familiar with County Kilkenny but have been to the city a good few times. It's an enjoyable place to visit, its centrepiece a proud, fabulously preserved castle that is thronged with visitors in summer. Kilkenny was once the seat of the Irish parliament, and there is a very definite sense of the city being a place apart.

The county is famous for its Lavistown cheese, a well-regarded semi-soft cheese that enjoys considerable success both at home and in England, where it is on sale in specialist shops. I prefer to use it for cooking rather than as part of a cheeseboard, as it can become quite crumbly when mature. It could form part of a picnic: I had a fabulous one that included Lavistown cheese – for one – in the grounds of the castle the first time I went there.

But if there needed to be only one reason for going to Kilkenny, it would have to be Zuni, a cutting-edge, cool and contemporary restaurant-townhouse in the middle of the medieval city. Whereas the rest of the city hasn't quite divorced itself from the fast-food joints that blight many Irish towns and cities, Zuni is pure 'kewl', a study in contemporary decor, with the emphasis on light and space.

If you stay there, you simply won't believe your eyes. The rooms are paragons of sophistication, fabulously well appointed. In fact, I wouldn't leave the room, save to have dinner in Zuni. And what a restaurant! Particularly admirable is the open-plan kitchen, which allows you to see everything that's going on. And what is going on is top-notch modern cooking, today's Irish cuisine with nods and influences from around the globe – I particularly like the Moroccan touches – all put together by the remarkable Maria Rafferty.

It's a near-flawless operation: the staff are friendly, the wine list superb, the food spot-on – totally assured and always on the right side of comfort, coupled with daring. Problem is, you'd miss it if you blinked, so inconspicuous is the premises. The bigger problem is: once you've found it, you'll never want to leave. A bit like Kilkenny itself, really.

There is a small production of veal in Kilkenny, though in fact it's more like *vittellone,* which is halfway between veal and beef. It's not really suitable for quickly cooked dishes but is ideal for braising, and therefore perfect for osso buco.

I first discovered osso buco (shin of veal) in France, not Italy. Many of the local restaurants where I lived had a habit of putting on a regional or foreign speciality every Saturday night: one week it could be couscous, the next cassoulet, and once a month osso buco, which they spelled 'bucco', an error I continued to make for years as a result.

I loved the dish, though these days it is often frowned upon because of both the BSE scare and the conditions under which veal is produced. Organic *vittellone* need not provoke any such qualms.

The best osso buco I ever ate was not in France, nor in Italy, but in Dublin. Johnny Cooke was brilliant at it, first in Polo One (RIP) and then in his own Cooke's Cafe, where a giant shin of beef, in an even bigger plate, was surrounded by sauce and vegetables, including leeks and peas. I liked the leeks so much I'm including them here, though they were not part of any osso buco recipe I used to do.

4 pieces of osso buco, around 300g each
Olive oil
3 carrots
4 sticks of celery
2 onions
The white of one leek
1 bottle of dry white wine
1 bouquet garni (bay, thyme and parsley tied together)
500g fresh peas (or Roma tinned petits pois)
Salt and pepper

First heat the oil in a frying pan over a gentle flame, then brown the meat on all sides. Season it well at the same time. When this is done, place the meat in a large oven dish or casserole (for oven use).

Finely dice the celery, carrots, onion and leeks and fry gently in the frying pan until they are a little browned. Then add all of them to the dish containing the veal shanks. Turn up the heat under the pan, then pour a third of the wine into the pan to deglaze it. Add this wine to the veal, along with the rest of the bottle.

Place the bouquet garni in the liquid and put the pan on the heat. Bring it to the boil, then reduce the flame to simmer. If the liquid does not cover the meat entirely, add water until the meat is fully immersed in the liquid.

At this point, place in an oven which has been preheated to around 180°C and leave for at least two hours. Check that the meat is ready: soft and coming away from the bone. If it isn't, return to the oven for at least another twenty-five minutes.

When ready to serve, bring to the simmer and add the peas until cooked. (If using tinned peas, reduce the sauce first and add them at the last moment, as they are already cooked.) The sauce will reduce while they are cooking.

Osso buco is traditionally served with *risotto alla milanese* (a recipe for rabbit risotto is given on page 230), potatoes or just rice. It is the only Italian *secondo* (main course) which is served with risotto. (Risotto is usually served as a starter.) Cover with finely chopped parsley before serving or, even better, *gremolata* (see below).

I love *gremolata* and I love it to be classic: parsley, lemon and garlic. I'm told you shouldn't mess with Italian food, and I try to adhere to that: such clever-clever concoctions as smoked-chilli *gremolata* are not for me.

In the north of Ireland, there is a tendency to find *gremolata* mixed with breadcrumbs and coated around meat or fish before it is deep-fried. What is the point? *Gremolata* – raw garlic, freshly chopped parsley and grated lemon peel – is one of the zingiest, most uplifting tastes around. Liberally applied to fish or white meats, it is a joy both to behold and to consume.

Personally I blame Robbie Millar for all the chefs who ever propagated the deep-fried-breadcrumby travesty: they all said they learned it in Shanks. To be fair to Robbie, he probably did it once as a culinary wink and probably did it brilliantly, but it illustrates the dangers of others, not quite so skilled, picking up a kitchen in-joke third-hand and passing it off as the real thing. Horsewhipping's too good for them.

This is *gremolata*. The McCoy.

Large bunch of fresh parsley, roughly chopped
    (Try and get the flat-leaf variety. If you don't come across
    it, try harder.)
1 garlic clove, peeled and finely chopped
Zest of 1 lemon

Mix all the ingredients thoroughly. The aroma alone is worth going to the small amount of trouble of making it. Apply liberally to the first passing fish you see.

WEXFORD

Wexford, I salute you. You are home to the Croghan Goat Farm and therefore to Mine-Gabhar, that amazing goat's cheese made by Dutchman Luc Van Kampen – and that's more than enough for me. Mine-Gabhar (the bane of many a non-Irish-speaking wait-ress's life) is a truly legendary cheese: it is rarely available in restau-rants – but all the more enjoyable for that when you do find it. This cheese, which is at once elegant, firm and seductively soft on the palate, is impossible to stop eating once you get your mitts on it. It is also a superb partner to a fascinating array of wines.

For a long time Wexford was somewhere to go on a drive to from Dublin, either for a weekend, for the world-renowned Opera Festival, or just for Sunday lunch. I remember well how it arrived in my conciousness in the mid-eighties when the words 'Wexford', 'Gorey' and 'Marlfield House' were interchangeable. It seemed as though all of Dublin society – most of them restaurant critics – decamped to Marlfield House every Sunday. You could then read of their escapades in the papers the following Sunday.

There is no doubt that, then as now, it was a lovely county to drive to, but these days it has much more to offer, in terms of products and outlets, as well as fine restaurants and country hotels. The county town, for example, is home to Green Acres, a beloved food and wine hall in North Main Street, in the county town. This 'food venue', established in 1860, is a treasure trove of esoteric wines, pâtés, chocolates and cheeses (get some Mine-Gabhar while you're there!). It also houses a coffee shop, where you can take the weight off your feet when you're shopped out. And pop up to Wallace's supermarket on Wellington Bridge for the best meat in the county.

Anyone who has driven the length of Wexford to get the ferry to France will of course know the joys of Kelly's Resort Hotel. Although it is also a marvellous place to stop over and spend some time, most of us will look forward simply to sampling the fare at its La Marine bistro prior to boarding the ferry. This spacious restaurant serves a variety of menus – from simple toasted sandwiches to full meals – at all times. The fresh fish from nearby Kilmore Quay – another great fishing village, where sublime fish and shellfish can be purchased – really ought to be sampled.

Kelly's also houses an elegant dining room with dedicated menus. The wine list here is simply superb: many of the wines are imported directly by the owners and are exclusive to the restaurant.

Should you be spending some time in the county, don't miss the beautifully appointed fishing village of Duncannon and its amazing restaurant, which goes by the unusual name of 'Squigl'. This is a superb seafood restaurant, to be spoken of in hushed tones. It is, quite simply, a little treasure: a lovely, warm and inviting place with excellent French-Mediterranean cooking. If you go there when the sun is out, you will find yourself transported.

Dunbrody House is one of Ireland's finest foodie hotels. It has the good fortune to be housed on the idyllic Hook Peninsula and is just fifteen minutes from Waterford city. As well as offering fine dining and stylish accommodation, it also runs one of the country's best-known cookery schools. The beginner or advanced cook alike can take a variety of courses, under the tutelage of head chef Kevin Dundon.

Wexford is often described as the sunny southeast. When the sun does shine, it can be just glorious: a joy to explore, and a haven of terrific eating places. Just don't get caught in the rain. If you do, remember that some Mine-Gabhar and a bottle of chilled, white, steely-tasting Châteauneuf-du-Pape would go a long way to providing superlative comfort.

Any dish that bears the name 'Parmentier' indicates the presence of potatoes. Antoine Auguste Parmentier was fed potatoes after having been captured by the Germans during the Seven Years War. He enthusiastically promoted the vegetable throughout France, using King Louis XVI as his publicist. Once it had secured his endorsement, the humble spud spread like wildfire throughout the kingdom; many of today's dishes, including *omelette Parmentière, potage Parmentier* and *hachis Parmentier* (see recipe on page 81) refer to the great spud-lover.

Omelette parmentière has saved my bacon on many an occasion after a night out on the tiles. One evening in Paris, I'd flown over to see the mighty Kassav' (a French Antillean band named after the root vegetable and West Indian staple, manioc, or cassava) and had partaken of too many rums and other splendid cocktails. The next day, dying, I spotted a restauarant which served only omelettes and which sounded like the very dab.

There must have been about forty different omelettes on the menu, but not my favourite, sautéed potato and Gruyère – though the ingredients firgured in the other concoctions. In two tics it was sorted: they made it for me and brought it to my table, along with a well-dressed green salad and lashings of Beaujolais.

10 eggs
A bunch of chives, finely chopped
Gruyère cheese, grated
6 medium potatoes, boiled, peeled and diced
Salt and pepper
Butter
Oil

Whisk the eggs together throughly, then add salt and pepper and a generous knob of butter. (The latter ingredient is a tip from Georges Blanc, the great chef from Vonnas: it will keep your omelette moist, should there be those among you who require their omelette more cooked than it really should be.)

Pour a little oil into a pan and heat until smoking. Add the potatoes and sauté them, browning them all over and seasoning as you go. Grate the Gruyère and finely chop the chives, adding them to the mixture.

When the potatoes are golden, add the egg mix to the pan, a wooden spoon in your hand. Don't just stand there, like an Englishman playing pinball! Get in there, pushing the mix towards the centre of the pan all the time. This will inject air and texture into the omelette as it cooks.

When the omelette is still a little runny, fold it over and slide it onto a preheated serving dish. Place in front of your guests, add a tossed green salad and consume. This is a great way of using up leftover potatoes and, if desired, leftover bacon or even fresh lardons.

There's a restaurant in Temple Bar which is the greatest of fun. Il
Baccaro is a cheap and cheerful Italian underground premises
where the wine seems to flow like water, from great big barrels of
the stuff poised invitingly on the counter. Cavernous and mysterious, it's just the place for a rowdy night out.

I'm told that, if you're female, the boy waiters are only gorgeous. They're certainly an interesting bunch, with strange facial
hair and mad Italian hand gestures.

If you're a man of sorts like myself, then I promise you the girl
waitresses are truly gorgeous. They have all been to the same waitress finishing school, which has taught them to make every single
man feel special, look them in the eye and smile suggestively at
them, even if they're silly old codgers. It's only at the moment
when you ask for *il conto,* and you're convinced you're going
home with at least one if not all of them, that they disappear and
you realise just how silly a codger you are.

Anyway, the food. They have this potato egg dish, an Italian
baked omelette called a *tortino.* I always begin a meal there with a
slice of it. It can be served hot or cold – or indeed enjoyed luke-
warm – and it's the biz. This is my version of it. (Mine is better
than theirs, though my looks simply cannot compete with theirs.)

6 eggs
Milk
Fresh sage leaves
4 large potatoes, peeled and sliced thinly
Nutmeg
Salt and pepper
Olive oil

Place all the sliced potatoes in a wide-bottomed pan with a splash
of olive oil and water to cover them and allow to simmer vigorously. Salt and pepper them, then add about half a dozen sage
leaves, either whole or julienned. Grate a little nutmeg into them
while they're cooking.

159

Whisk the eggs together thoroughly, add salt and a generous amount of freshly ground black pepper, plus a glass of milk.

When the potatoes have absorbed all the liquid and are almost cooked, add the egg mixture and stir briefly away from the sides into the centre of the pan. Then transfer to a hot oven for about fifteen minutes, keeping an eye on it.

The *tortino* will rise, will brown on top, will look utterly fabulous. It is then ready for eating, or it can be allowed to cool and eaten later. It will not stick to the bottom and can be plated by turning it upside-down onto a serving dish. The underside will also look most appetising.

Although you could add other ingredients, I feel that nothing beats the simplicity and perfection of potatoes, sage and egg.

MUNSTER

Time now for a little rant, methinks. Not, gentle reader – and especially those gentle readers from Waterford – a rant about Waterford, town or county, but a rant in general abouts chefs and 'cheffing'. A FAQ, if you will, to borrow from internet-speak. It is prompted by an incident this every morning with a taxi driver where I, about to strike up conversation with a couple of ill-thought-out questions, was pre-empted by a sudden statement. 'The two questions I hate most,' he ranted, 'are, "Are you busy?" and "Are you long started?"' – the very two questions I was about to ask him. I sheepishly chose silence as the better option.

Every profession gets its regularly asked questions. As I have already written, I used to hear the expression 'It's a good complaint' twenty times a day and more for ten very long years every time I remarked that we were busy in the restaurant. But, as a perceived member of the cheffing fraternity, I never get invited anywhere because of one of the supposed myths about us: that we're critical. Me, critical?

With some honourable exceptions in the last twelve months, nobody ever wants to have me round for dinner. They all say the same thing: 'I'm not going to cook for you!' Now, I think I speak for all chefs when I say that we would just love to be asked round for a bite and an oul' glass of something. Whatever you may think, we are not there to criticise, and have no intention of passing comment on your food, your culinary dexterity or any other aspect of your hospitality. In fact, the simpler the better. Wasn't it the greatest chef of all, Escoffier, who proclaimed: *Faites simple*?

Any chef worth his salt loves to eat, enjoy good company and share good times. I swear to God, we are great guests: please just give us that chance. It's not as if we will otherwise starve, obviously, but a chef on his night off would love to be invited into the home of others, just for a little pampering. We will be grateful, will flatter, will surely help with the washing up. We will tell customer jokes and stories from the kitchen – and that'll be great fun.

The other thing that we hear time and time again is the classic customer worry: 'Should I have the temerity to send my steak back to be cooked more? Will it be spat upon?' Ah, now here, will ye stop? That sort of thing just doesn't happen, and if it ever did, it's a practice that has long since been confined to the kitchen dustbins. I have never, ever, witnessed it, not in twenty years of working in a great deal of kitchens, whether I was in charge or not. I have never seen a steak dragged on the ground, abused, stood on – or any other of the silly things I hear or read about in dopey books or magazine articles. That really is fiction. No chef would contemplate doing such a thing, and no commis would dare do such a thing in front of his chef.

What is certainly true, however, is that we do not understand the 'well-done steak'. We search high and low to find the best suppliers, the people who will hang the meat correctly. We grill and fry with care, we confection the best sauces. It is therefore difficult to comprehend why a customer will pay us effectively to destroy the meat and take away that which makes each of us unique: the individual skill of cooking, that sleight-of-hand that belongs to no other. A well-done steak can be cooked by anyone, for the result will be the same, and the customer might as well stay at home and carbonise his steak there, saving himself quite a few euro in the process.

I have been in some kitchens where the words 'cremated', 'burnt' and so on have been programmed into the electronic order machine specifically for the steak orders. I find it very strange and difficult to fathom, but while it may from time to time provoke derision – often a source of much-needed comic relief in the middle of a busy service – it in no way attracts stupid or dangerous practices.

Mind you, in my time, when faced with the well-done steak that needs further incineration for Table 12, I have instructed the commis to 'Stick it into the oven, go on holiday to Barbados and expedite it on return – it will surely be ready then.' A fine example of my ready and all-consuming sledgehammer wit. Much laughter ensues, etc.

Another thing concerning the 'shteak' is the small matter of condiments in Ireland; this problem does not appear to be readily comprehended. Mustard and suchlike is just that – a condiment, to be enjoyed with a grilled and otherwise unadorned steak. It is bizarre, to the say the least, how we spend all afternoon making rich red-wine sauces, reducing stocks, walking on eggs where sauce bearnaise and derivatives are concerned (superb pun very much intended) or melting the finest of cheeses, before finally arriving at the *monter au beurre* stage, then admiring our work, the elegance of viscosity, the shine of glaze, only to have someone demand mustard, rendering the sauce pointless, undoing all the hard work, in a single phrase revealing that they don't appreciate what you've been up to, they want their mustard anyhow.

It's at a time like this that you begin to appreciate the sauce-on-the-side merchant, that other no-good son-of-a-gun! Why the hell did you come out anyway, we hiss under our breaths, messing with my presentation, wreckin' me buzz, you nefarious nuisance? Get up the yard! Then you remember: the customer is king, and you're only as good as your last meal. You calm down and move on to the next table.

Mind you, it isn't only the customers who get in the way of a seamless service, though they will of course nightly get the blame. A pet bugbear of mine was the perennial infighting between kitchen and front-of-house, a tedious, time-wasting nonsense. Most of the time both sides get on with the job and spend time in each other's company after service; and there is of course the eternal intrigue as to who is doing what to whom. But every so often tempers will flare as to a misplaced order, a delay on a table, a dish sent back.

This is, I suppose, inevitable, but what I hate is the discussion that then ensues. I say: look, lads, put it right. Make good whatever is causing the problem now and then discuss it at the end of the night. Try to keep the customer satisfied. The dawdling and pointless discussions that I have witnessed have been infuriating, because no amount of gawking at the wrong sauce will make it the right one, nor will fruitless searching for a lost docket help get the food any more quickly to the table.

Then of course there is the case of the salty soup: you have really got to be careful with those over-enthusiastic commis chefs just itching to spoil the broth. There is always one, confident in his enthusiasm but with yet a lot to learn, who will throw pepper-corns into the soup before 'blitzing' it. (We love the word 'blitz-ing', as we love all our other awfully macho terms. Blitzing is blending the soup with a hand-held professional blender, which can do umpteen litres at a go. Know what we call it? A gun.)

Watch this commis: as the soup is handed back to him by the waiter or waitress, he will first of all state that 'It's not too salty.' Now watch. Forced by the wait-person to confront the alleged over-salty soup as being just that, he will lift a wooden spoon (now banned, thankfully), sip a little of the soup, and triumphantly pontificate: 'See, it's not too salty at all.' Well, tish and pish. You cannot possibly taste a soup properly in such conditions. I always used to wait until after service, sit the little blighter down, and make him taste at least three or four tablespoonfuls from a bowl-ful similar to that which the customer got: in other words, to taste it in the same circumstances as the upstart customer. The saltiness will manifest itself after the third palateful, and the customer, that much-misunderstood individual, will be proved right.

You can at least remedy the situation by simmering the soup with umpteen potatoes cut in half thrown into it, to absorb the excess salt. Handfuls of parsley will also go some way to correct-ing the imbalance, as will roast garlic cloves. But for blitzed pep-percorns, dream on: there is nothing you can do. Just don't pep-per soup in the first place. The taste gets everywhere, it spreads around the mouth like a malign computer virus, it renders the soup inedible, it then renders the rest of the meal inedible because, unless the customer is prepared to eat coconut, drink yoghurt or swallow a few slices of banana in the middle of their expected ele-gant meal, they will be unable to taste squat. Ever again. I repeat, don't pepper soup in the first place. Thus endeth the rant.

I am filled with admiration for the people who work in the industry. Those who do it night after night uncomplainingly, working dreadfully long hours, battling against docket after dock-et, effortlessly turning out perfect dishes, 'cleaning down' and try-ing to find a modicum of social life somewhere. They get up the hill every single night, then march down and begin again the very next day. I can't do it. Or rather, I can no longer do it. Being a TV chef or pontificating about food on the steam radio is much more my line. I think at some point I got kitchen-happy, just could no longer stand the noise of the place, with its constant slamming of pots, pans and other shiny metal things into one another, the macho yells of 'Pick up!' and 'Service!', '*Ça marche!*' and '*On enlève, siou plait!*' What a big girl's blouse.

*

I think that the Tannery Restaurant in Waterford is one of Ireland's finest. It is rare that one can gain an insight into the raison d'être of a given establishment long before going there, but the gentle scribblings of its owner-chef, Paul Flynn, week after week in his Saturday column in the *Irish Times* filled me with admiration for his writing and the odour of his food, which leapt off the page as though it were scratch 'n' sniff. Above all, it made me want to go to his restaurant, then and there.

This evident brilliance was eventually proved by a visit there on my birthday some three years ago, but the reasons for it are hard work and a career at the top. Paul first spent almost nine years with the renowed Nico LaDenis at his restaurant Chez Nico in London, where Paul eventually became head chef at just twenty-three years of age. Eventually, wishing to return to Ireland, he accepted the position of head chef at La Stampa, one of the finest restaurants in Dublin. La Stampa then enjoyed one of its best periods and in 1993 was named Restaurant of the Year in Ireland by Egon Ronay. By 1997, Paul had returned home to Dungarvan and opened his own place, the Tannery, in a disused leather factory.

Since then the restaurant has been showered with accolades, the most recent of which is 'Jameson Restaurant of the Year'. It was thus with high expectations that I went to eat there that September night some years back. The dining room, on the first floor, was one of the most sophisticated I have ever seen: it was cool and utterly contemporary, and had an efficient, slick, yet warm Irish service that was always on hand but otherwise invisible.

It goes without saying that the food was first-class, but more than that, it was clever. What impressed me was not just the cutting-edge items on the oh-so-modern menu but also the reinven-

167

tion of classics like steak and mash. This dish was here deconstructed and reassembled in a way that was not just pleasing to the eye but which contained every single item a diner of the old school could want: here in one corner were the mushrooms, there the onion rings, over there the peas, in the middle the steak – in this instance, well-done. But presented in this fashion, the kitchen could have fun with the dish, previously the bane of my existence, while satisfying their less adventurous customers.

How could I resist a starter such as glazed onion tart with soft Dromana cheese – the nucleus of the dish being the onion tart, a favourite of mine since forever, the twist of the Irish cheese lending this delicate Alsace favourite a touch of a soft Irish day? It was a fight between that and crab crème brulée with pickled cucumber and melba toast, which, when tasted, adjusted my long-standing hatred of the cucumber (fit only for blue movies, I say). It was all my kind of food: caramelised belly pork, sea bream with fab crushed potatoes, and then, sexiest of all, roast and confit of chicken with lemon cannellini bean stew, roasted garlic and *boulangère* potatoes, a dish that should either be knighted or have sainthood conferred upon it.

The evening was delirious and is now a blur; there was a warm burnish to the restarant which I insist was there, despite copious amounts of my favourite Burgundy. You really must go there if you want to try one of Ireland's leading restaurants. While waiting, do also buy a copy of Paul's book, *An Irish Adventure with Food*.

Finally, I have two things to thank Paul Flynn for. First, I was there on my birthday, and so thanks for the cake, Paul. Secondly, thanks for gracing this book with one of your recipes, given below.

COURGETTE AND BROAD-BEAN RISOTTO
WITH TOMATO, MOZZARELLA AND BASIL

One of the classic flavour combinations. If you can't get good plum tomatoes, used canned instead – infinitely better than those unripe pretend tomatoes.

1.5 litres (2.5 pints) chicken stock (from a stock cube is fine)
1 tablespoon olive oil
40g (or 1.5oz) butter
1 onion, finely chopped
400g (or 14oz) Arborio (risotto) rice
150ml (or quarter-pint) dry white wine
450g (or 1lb) ripe plum tomatoes, seeded and chopped
       or a 400g (14oz) can chopped tomatoes
450 g (or 1lb) broad beans, podded
2 courgettes, thinly sliced
Handful fresh basil leaves, torn, plus extra leaves to garnish
1 buffalo mozzarella, diced into 1cm (half-inch) cubes
Salt and freshly ground black pepper
Freshly grated Parmesan to garnish (optional)

Serves 4

Pour the stock into a pan and bring to a gentle simmer. Heat a separate large, heavy-based pan. Add the olive oil and 25g (1oz) of the butter. Once the butter has stopped foaming, add the onion and sauté over a gentle heat for three minutes. Add the rice and cook for a further two minutes, making sure every grain is coated with the oil and butter. Pour in the wine and allow to cook until it is completely absorbed. Add the tomatoes and cook for another minute. Stir a ladleful of stock into the rice mixture and allow it to be almost completely absorbed before adding another ladleful. Continue to cook for another fifteen to twenty minutes until the rice is al dente. Season to taste.

Meanwhile, bring a large pan of salted water to the boil. Add the

169

broad beans and cook for about two minutes or until tender. Drain and refresh in a large bowl of iced water, then slip the beans out of their skins. Add the courgettes to the pan and blanch for one minute, then drain and refresh as before. Tip on to kitchen paper and allow to dry completely.

Remove the cooked risotto from the heat and stir in the blanched broad beans and courgettes, torn basil and mozzarella. Divide among warmed, wide-rimmed serving bowls and garnish with some fresh basil leaves and Parmesan, if desired. Serve at once.

French cuisine is the cooking that I know best. It is the one that first inspired me to take up the pan, but even more importantly, the one that taught me how to eat. I am also very lucky to have known most of the major regional variants of French cuisine and to have visited most of the regions that nurture it. One region I love but have seldom visited is Alsace. It appeals to me, as it would to most people, because of its quaint image of jolly little taverns along the *route du vin,* all serving hearty fare and quaffable jugs of the local *edelzwicker.* Scratch the surface and you will find Germanic-looking fare such as choucroute, Germanic-sounding wine such as Riesling and, of course, Germanic-tasting beer such as Fischer Gold. Delve a little deeper, and you will find that the food, though hearty, is subtle and imbued with Gallic flair, the wine fragrant yet bone-dry, and the beer – well, there's no way that that could ever be as good as it is in Germany.

Alsace has changed hands between France and Germany several times; while the local patois and surnames owe much to the fatherland, the outlook is now unmistakably French. I think I've only ever been to Alsace once, and that was to Strasbourg, home to Europe and to many fine restaurants and a famous catering college. I never made it inland into the little wine villages but I will someday, for I've grown to know this part of France's cuisine very well since its fame has spread all over that nation. Thus the famous *choucroute* – or what the Germans call sauerkraut – has become one of the country's most famous dishes, alongside bouillabaisse, cassoulet and indeed *coq au vin.* The Alsace version of *choucroute* has been pampered and refined to such a degree that it can be found made with Riesling or even champagne; one can enjoy in many establishments a *choucroute de la mer,* or seafood *choucroute.*

This recipe is one of the glories of Alsace, alongside such delights as *kugelhopf* and *flammekuche.* It has remained a firm favourite of mine for many years. (I believe it was one of John Hume's too when he was serving over there.) The tart has the same pastry as quiche Lorraine – but there the similarity stops. Unlike the quiche, no egg whites are used in the mixture and therefore it does not rise – and it certainly does not fall either. So, while it can be eaten as an oven-to-table dish, it can also be enjoyed cold the next day, or even gently reheated. It remains moist, because only egg yolks are used, and best of all, it is a dish that can be enjoyed by meat-eaters and vegetarians alike – as long as the latter will eat eggs and cream.

But for all that, the greatest thrill has to be when it is taken out of the oven and placed before your guests. Golden-brown on top, with a wonderful swirly pattern created by the cooked onion slices, the smell is to die for. It can be served as a first course by itself or perhaps as a supper dish accompanied by a crisp green salad. If you follow this recipe to the letter, you will get a perfect result every time.

for the pastry:
250g plain flour
100g butter, cubed
Salted water
1 egg

for the tart:
6 onions
Butter
Bay leaves
Flour
6 egg yolks
250ml cream
Salt
Cracked black pepper
Freshly grated nutmeg

In a bowl, combine the butter with the flour until you obtain a sandy, golden texture. Add the whole egg and then the salted water until you have formed a malleable dough. Place this in the fridge while you are making the rest of the dish. Peel the onions, cut them in half and then thinly slice them so that all the slices are crescent-shaped. Melt a generous knob of butter in the pan over a low heat. Stir in the onions with a handful of bay leaves and stir all the while until they become transparent, taking care not to let them colour. When they are transparent, dust lightly with the flour, which will absorb all the butter in the pan, and leave for another two or three minutes so that the flour cooks. At this point, remove the pan from the heat to finish the mixture. (If you leave it over the flame, it will curdle.) Add the egg yolks to the onions and combine thoroughly, then add the cream slowly until you have formed a thick but liquid mixture. At this point, add the salt, pepper and nutmeg. Taste, and adjust the seasoning if necessary.

Roll out the pastry wide enough to fill your tart dish – a professional one with a removeable bottom is best – and make sure it's thin so that it will cook crisp. When that is done, add the mixture to it, spreading it all over the base and up the sides. If you like, grate some more nutmeg on top or sprinkle on some more cracked black pepper. Trim away the extra pastry from the sides, place in the centre of an oven preheated to about 200°C and leave to cook for about twenty minutes to half an hour. Keep an eye on it and turn the oven up to 360°C at least once while cooking to get it browned equally on all sides. Remove from the oven and serve immediately; it can also be eaten cold the next day.

If you want a nice salad with it, mix three parts groundnut oil to one part white-wine vinegar, with a dollop of good French mustard. Whisk until emulsified, add some crisp green leaves, salt and pepper the leaves to taste, and toss. Wash the tart down with an equally crisp Riesling or Tokay d'Alsace and, as they say over there, *Bon appétit,* or, even more locally, *A guata!*

You'd walk quickly in the door, take in the bright, white open kitchen, and he'd usually be standing there, a confident grin that said 'Bring those dockets on', a John Lennon stance, a cheery nod of recognition. It was Cooke's Café in the early nineties, all *kalamata* olives, angel-hair pasta, the 'various oils and balsamic vinegar' that trumpeted the 'new age, new style' house slogan. He, however, was not Johnny Cooke: he was Harry McKeogh, for many years the main man in the kitchen.

At this point, let us have a respectful silence to remember some of the triumphs from the once-ever-so-trendy Cooke's: the buzz of long Saturday lunches, not to mention the ladies-what-lunch ethos of midweek, Marianne Faithfull sitting in the corner – still a fine thing, with, as it happens, her angel hair, and a woman who could sing to me in broken English any day – and superlative dishes like the thick, chunky John Dory with pink grapefruit and capers that you'd drool endlessly about, with a side of angel hair, natch.

After the demise of Cooke's (now recently arisen from its ashes in exactly the same premises), I didn't see Harry for years. I was living elsewhere, and I assumed he was cheffing anonymously somewhere, until the day I suddenly spotted him, complete with the aforementioned confident grin, adorning the cover of *The Bridgestone Irish Food Guide*. Even then, I thought that they'd chosen one of our more photogenic chefs for their cover. It was to be some time before I realised that he'd opened his own purpose-built restaurant down the country. (Opening the book and actually reading it helps, of course.)

'Down the country' turned out to be County Tipperary. Or perhaps not. Opinion is divided on the issue: some say the restaurant is in Clare; others that it's firmly in Tipp. In any case, it's in the most beautiful setting, overlooking the River Shannon on the Ballina side of Killaloe. It was with great pleasure that I renewed my acquaintance with Harry there on a couple of memorable occasions.

The outstanding interior boasts plate-glass windows, which, if you can tear yourself away from the food on your plate, afford stunning views of the river and of the village of Killaloe. The elegant bar area is a place for taking an aperitif or digestif in the most comfortable of leather armchairs, while contemplating the menus and wine list. In fine weather, a meal can be taken outside, overlooking the Shannon.

Harry kindly lent me his kitchen – and some of his wilder mushrooms – for one of my kamikaze three-minute TV dishes on my first visit. It was his menu and the cooking of his chef Mark Anderson that prompted my second. I was never quite able to shake off the memory of my first meal there, and particularly Harry's use of those little green *feves* (young broad beans) that I just love, daintily arranged in the lightest of foaming sauces. The menu was just too good, too light, too well-executed for you not to want a second crack at it. I have to confess that, while in the region one day, I deliberately contrived to miss my flight to Paris so that I could stay the night and eat there.

The restaurant, now under chef Mark Anderson, has one of the simplest yet most innovative menus in the country, backed up by a magnificent wine list. Organic produce, the fruits of our countryside, the fish of our seas – all are treated with utter respect, imagination, and a culinary legerdemain that outshines the decor, the elegance, the setting – well, to this tummy anyway. To the Cherry Tree go, and have anything with those green *feves* in it.

It was a cousin who first brought me to Tipp, when he was living in Clonmel, 'the Honey Meadow'. I loved going there, tasting Beamish and Hoffman's (two stouts widely available in the Midlands) for the first time, and quickly exhausting the town's rich collection of traditional Irish Chinese restaurants. I assumed that this was it as far as the endeavours of food went in Tipperary, and put up gratefully with the below-par cooking of the average rural Chinese when I was not cooking the fresh fish that my cousin oftimes caught locally. He is a keen fisherman; I am not.

*

One memorable weekend I was told that we were going to Cashel to eat, and that a table was booked, for Saturday night at eight thirty, when the two-point-four kids were in bed for the night. The name of the place – Chez Hans – didn't exactly fill me with great expectations, since Hans, Fritz and Günter have never been synonymous with the bearable lightness of eating. This was long ago, in the eighties, and I was far from prepared for the reality of this lovely restaurant, which, to add to its charm, is located in a converted church.

But read carefully. I will never forget, not to my dying day, my first mouthful in Chez Hans. It was a garden-vegetable soup – probably described more florally than that, but made with garden spring vegetables and garden herbs. It was exquisite, it was bliss, it was a bowl of liquid heaven. After that, helped by oysters and Dopff and Irion's Riesling, the meal got even better.

No doubt at this point I should point out how lovely Cashel is – how impressive and imposing its magnificent rock is. Don't mind that. I think only of the oysters, the lamb, the veal, the lobster, the wines, all the great things about Chez Hans, where our national products are cooked in a manner that befits them.

Since that first impressive visit, I've been back any number of times. It is true and fair to say that the cooking would be perceived as that of a bygone era – sumptuous and luxurious products, with sauces that are rich and hearty – and may have fallen out of favour elsewhere. But it is precisely this – the roaring fires, the old-style decor of high ceilings and huge windows – that makes Chez Hans so attractive, and the setting demands a menu of unalterable style, now superbly executed by Hans's son Jason Matthia.

If you're going there, note that Chez Hans has now spawned a little bistro – a Hans-ette, if you will, right next door. The food is simpler, fun and friendly, perfect for when you're passing through Cashel on your way further down the country.

Do stop and admire that Rock, though.

FILET DE BOEUF 'HERMITAGE'

I recently came across two recipes in a magazine which had done an article on me, complete with photographs. The text and photos made me laugh: I am described as a 'tough-looking northerner' and the photo is of me with my habitual Armagnac in one hand (something I no longer drink), my flock-of-seagulls hairstyle – and only the one chin. The recipes too made me laugh: one of them is certainly a bit dated.

*

'This dish is so named because of the famous, delicous and expensive Rhône wine that I used to make it. Of course, any good Rhône wine would do, but the appellation "Hermitage" would then be disallowed.' (Ooh! Wasn't I a stand-up guy?) 'As for the sauce, it is a variant of a *bordelaise* or *marchand de vin* sauce.'

Bottle of Hermitage or other Rhône wine
Beef stock
1 fillet steak per person
6 shallots
Sugar cubes
Butter

for the sauce:
There are two essential ingredients: a good beef stock and a bottle of 'Hermitage' from E. Guigal.

The stock must be reduced considerably over a high heat until it attains a syrupy consistency. At the same time, the wine must be reduced by one third and fortified by the additon of two sugar cubes and six chopped shallots.

Add the wine to the stock via a strainer. Unlike in a *marchand de vin* sauce, the shallots are removed, leaving only their flavour: in a sauce of this calibre, nothing should detract from the brilliant

177

colour that the sauce will have. (It seems I really used to go to these lengths.)

Now add a couple of generous knobs of unsalted butter, swirling the pot over a high heat but without letting it boil. The butter will finish the sauce both in taste and looks, imparting a beatiful sheen. Season well.

to prepare the fillet:
Allow one fillet steak per person. Each should be sliced into medallions, grilled quickly under a hot flame, or dry-fried on a non-stick pan.

The article goes on to say: 'Arrange the medallions attractively on a servicing dish, with the sauce underneath', to which I say, no kidding? The dish has a garnish of potato, ratatouille and green beans. Fifteen years later, I say blow the ratatouille, and especially the silly-looking carrot fanned in a very boring fashion.

PAUPIETTE DE CRABE

I have no recollection of this dish, but it sounds fun enough, for old times' sake. Apparently I dictated: 'This is again a very simple dish. It is a delicious combination of filo pastry and crabmeat. Buy the filo pastry at a reputable delicatessen, such as the excellent Magill's of Clarendon Street, Dublin' (which is still there, folks).

300g crabmeat
Saffron
White wine
Filo pastry
1 leek
Butter

Serves 4

Warm the crab-flesh in a pan with a little saffron and white wine. Place the crabmeat on flat sheets of filo pastry which are then formed into 'pouches' and tied at the open end with a 'lace' cut from the green part of a leek. Brush these pouches with melted butter and place in a very hot oven. Bake for five to ten minutes until golden. It is a good idea to prepare a little sauce to complement the *paupiettes* – nothing too grand. Try a reduction of white wine and shallots simply thickened with cream and a couple of strands of saffron to give a good yellow hue.

*

I note two things when rereading the above recipe. First, I am surprised at the use of the word *'paupiette'* in the title: they should really be called *'bourses'* or *'aumônières'*, for 'purses'. Secondly, I remember the problems we had when removing them from the oven: the sides and top would be golden and crisp but not the underside, which had not cooked and would be soggy from the filling. Simple solution: gently fry in a little butter in a pan before serving and the underside will crispen up too.

I'll be killed if I don't put this in. Chicken fried rice is one of my favourite things, a comfort food of utter simplicity that is a pleasure to put together and a great way of using up leftovers. It is also as much a pick-me-up, I feel, as that other great Oriental dish, chicken noodle soup.

I always have cooked rice and cooked potatoes in my fridge, as they can be turned into so many great little dishes with a minimum of fuss and preparation: rice salad, potato salad (with mustard vinaigrette and hot sausage), omelettes, *tortine* and so on. Every kitchen these days should have ingredients and condiments such as peanut oil, Japanese soy sauce, good Dijon mustard, white-wine or spirit vinegar, hot pepper sauce, and *nam pla* or fish sauce. With elements like these, great, tasty food is never far away.

There are umpteen variations on chicken fried rice, and no one recipe is definitive. This one comes from the mother of one of my many Internet/mobile phone contacts, someone to whom I've been 'speaking' for years but who I have never met – a typical arangement in our brave new cyberworld. Text messaging has been a source of many such recipes for me over the years, such as the recipe for a delicious potato, rosemary and onion pizza, so typical of Sicily, sent to me via concatenated SMS from a beach on the island by an Italian child psychiatrist. (No jokes about my needing one, please.) You can cook this dish in a wide-bottomed frying pan, but use a wok if you have one.

> 250g cold leftover rice or rice cooked for the purpose,
>   refreshed in cold running water.
> 2 cloves of garlic, roughly chopped
> 1 red chilli, deseeded and chopped
> Sesame oil
> Fish sauce to taste
> Soy sauce
> Pinch of white pepper
> 3 eggs

Leftover roast chicken stripped from the carcass and sliced thinly, or raw breast of chicken, cut into strips
Mangetout, sliced lengthwise into thin slivers
Tin of peas, preferably Roma petits pois
Tin of sweetcorn
Chinese sausage, sliced in thin circles
    (available in Chinese supermarkets such as the Asia Market in Drury Street, Dublin)
Red pepper, diced
Sliced ham or roast pork

to garnish:
Scallions and coriander leaves
Cashew nuts if desired

Heat the sesame oil over a high heat, add the garlic, the diced red pepper and the chopped chilli and stir quickly. If using raw chicken, add it at this point, but if using leftover coooked chicken, keep it back for the time being. When the chicken is part-cooked, add the eggs directly to the mixture one by one, and beat them in with a wooden spoon. Then add the rice and stir vigorously, breaking up any larger bits of cooked egg.

At this point, add the other ingredients – that is, the cooked chicken if not using raw, the Chinese sausage (sliced in thin circles), the corn and peas, and so on – keeping a third of the sliced mangetout back for garnish. Stir well. Remove the white ends from the scallions, cut them in half and add them to the hot rice mixture, then finely chop the green leaf and reserve it for garnish.

When cooked, season to taste with a splash of fish sauce and soy sauce (these are used instead of salt) and the white pepper. Place on a hot serving dish, mould attractively with the flat of the wooden spoon, and sprinkle with the cashew nuts (if using), coriander leaves (chopped) and scallions.

Add people, a few beers, soy sauce on the table and a little chilli oil. Children will enjoy this too (but go easy on the chilli for them).

CORK

I first went to Cork more than thirty years ago: I remember it so well because in those simpler times it came as a shock that there was a second (or indeed a third) city in Ireland that had wide thoroughfares and double-decker buses. I simply had no idea. Of course, I confess that in those days I wasn't going to Cork for food, rather for a feed of drink and a rake of tunes in bars. I remember our older companion, Basil, shocking us with his demand that we go for a fine steak first because 'If you were going to put all that drink in you, you should have a good meal first': words which more often than not come from myself these days when in lecturing mode. But impecunious students that we were then – I think I was over on loan from Wales for the week – the admonishment fell on surprised ears. Nevertheless, a steak was found, and rather good it was too. Thus began, albeit tenuously, a relationship with Cork, city and county, and an association in my mind of Cork with food.

One other thing that shocked was the local tongue. I remember well being in a bar in the centre of town – An Bodhrán, if my failing memory continues to serve me betimes – and hearing ''Ow are 'oo'' for the first time. After a fruitless half-hour of Corkese, I had to implore my interlocutors to speak Irish to me so that we might understand each other. This worked, despite my having a less-than-nodding acquaintance with the Munster dialect of Gaeluinn: in my first times in Cork, Irish was infinitely preferable to my ear than the thick emulsion that was the sweet English of Cork. Now, of course, linguistic sophisticate that I am, I lap up that local dialect.

Trips to Cork became more frequent after I settled in Dublin: these visits were more for the food and a change of culinary scenery than anything else. I loved the strange layout of the city, and discovering its odd little alleyways, with their promise of undiscovered eating houses – like the Oyster Tavern, a veritable institution, which I thought was bliss back then.

It was in the late eighties and early nineties that the city of

Cork seemed to find its gastronomic feet. Up in Dublin, we'd always heard of the likes of Michael Ryan's Arbutus Lodge and seen it written about in glowing terms. Then, however, other things started to happen – like Michael Clifford relocating to Cork and doing smashing things with the county's Clonakilty black pudding. Or like the buzz-filled brasserie, Isaac's, which we in Dublin envied – and still do. Or, even more recently, like Seamus O'Connell and his crazy Ivory Tower, with its stunning food – in fact, its utterly mad food that works, such as John Dory with banana ketchup. And of course, Seamus himself: only in Ireland, and then perhaps only in Cork, could I have a chat with a flame-haired American chef with an Irish accent who would turn out to have been responsible for some of the most remarkable desserts I have ever tasted in my once-favourite restaurant in Lyon, in France, La Tour Rose, where Seamus was pastry chef way back in 1986.

Most of all, Cork is also home to Ireland's best vegetarian restaurant. Café Paradiso is a small, unassuming place where both the food and the service are exemplary. The food is so good that you may cheerfully forget that meat ever existed. I have to get one thing off my chest here: I don't care one whit for their anti-French wine policy, though I respect it. But, er, that's it. The food is simply superb, confident and assured, displaying a blistering comprehension of ingredients, textures and flavours. And though I say this, I have absolutely no recollection of what I ate there, simply because I do not have the culinary imagination that can produce or recollect food of this flair and know-how. It's food that is extremely clever, without ever being smart-alecky. My own food is of a much more prosaic nature: I am pleased to say it often gets to the point, but equally often it is, as the saying goes, 'Close, but no cigar.'

Denis Cotter, the owner and chef of Café Paradiso, turns out astonishing food day after day without a trace of meat or fish near it. In fact, he turns it out even when he's not in his restaurant, and while doing all this he also manages to write great cookbooks. In fact, let's just finish this eulogy with the information that, at the time of writing, he has just won the 'Best Vegetarian Cookbook in the World' award in Barcelona. And this clever lad has his restaurant in Cork. You have to go there.

With restaurants like these, what then can I say of the most fabulous covered market in Ireland, which is just off the main drag in the city centre? If there is one reason for going to Cork, it is to visit the thrilling English market, which they are very fortunate to have all to themselves. Every city should have the like, but for the moment we must envy the Corkonians in their lovely city for this market, filled with fresh meat and fish, local specialities such as drisheen and tripe (if you have the stomach for them), fruit, vegetables, spices, wines, cheeses, olives and breads. And then, of course, there is 'Mr Bell's', where, to my utter delight, I found a bottle of my favourite Hot Pepper Sauce from Trinidad, from shelves bulging with hot sauces from all over the world. But mere description can do no justice to the sheer pleasure of strolling around the English Market's food-laden stalls: I urge you to see it for yourself.

Much as I have a hankering for the fish stalls, one of my favourite outlets is the aptly named 'On the Pig's Back' stall, run by the gorgeous Isabelle Sheridan from Tours. Isabelle offers in-house specialities of *saucisson,* hams, pâtés and terrines, not to mention fabulous foie gras and cheeses – and don't miss the *saucisson aux cepes* or the *terrine de porc aux pruneaux*. Everything is home-made or sourced from the finest suppliers: Michael Ryan's Arbutus bread, fine French and Irish cheeses and, lately, fresh truffles imported from Italy, along with truffle-related specialities such as truffle butter.

If all this ambling around the English Market has you salivating and hungry, you can always repair upstairs and sample the excellent fare at the Farmgate Café: a sister establishment to the Farmgate restaurant and food emporium in Midleton in east Cork (where you can also sample the fancy whiskey).

*

Of course, it isn't possible to visit Cork without becoming aware of the existence of Kinsale, a charming town which was in the vanguard of good food long before Cork, and which gives the impression of being one big restaurant. For me, discovering Kinsale, way back in the 1980s, was like discovering France for the first time (a whole country devoted to food) or Trinidad (an entire island devoted to partying) or even Singapore (an island state devoted to boys' toys). And discover it I did – though not without incident.

I was determined to eat my way around the town in one weekend; this was impossible, of course, but I gave it my best shot. It seemed incredible then that Ireland could have a small town, with its extremely attractive and neat little streets, that seemed to be completely given over to food. I began in the Blue Haven on Friday: I still remember the salmon *faela* I had there: a confection of baked salmon in pastry with crab and spinach. But it was a marvellous beginning to the weekend and twenty years later the memory shines on. We tried the Spinnaker, and it too was grand, and then on our last night, we asked locals for their idea of somewhere else that might be equally grand and that we could sample. We were told 'Man Friday', and drove up a steep hill to it.

Now here's something I'm not likely to forget. It had huge paving stones as steps leading down to it: I'm glad to say I've seen them commented on in descriptions of the place elsewhere. Twenty years ago, filled with enthusiasm for food – and more than a little starving – I flew down those steps, determined to secure a table for two. As I careered front-door-wards, I felt a crack in my knee, somersaulted, and landed not just on my back but upside down, like a scene from a bad British sitcom.

The proprietress looked at me sternly as I, upside down and in absolute agony, tried to smile, grin, or at least look affable. Most of all, I was keen to appear to be neither drunk nor a complete loony. 'Have you got a table for two?' I asked, wincing. To her credit, the proprietress took this wholly novel way of reserving a table in her stride and said there was just one left and that she would hold it for me for five minutes. I managed to pick myself up, crawled back up those steps, told my companion (who now also thought I was a loony) that we had a table, limped back down the steps, negotiated the door, and dragged myself to the table. By now, of course, my appetite was gone, and even a bottle of Chateau Giscours '76 (yeah, yeah, it was cheap in those days) couldn't help. I had a ghastly final evening in Kinsale as my knee filled with water and blood and swelled to gigantic proportions, but it is a tribute to the Man Friday and to Kinsale that I returned many times thereafter. I don't run about the place any more, mind you.

In the twenty-first century, Kinsale hasn't changed very much, I'm happy to say, but it does have one new addition to its scene, which has caused grown men to sob at the thought of it and grown chefs to stop and talk to one another civilly. Let me tell you about it. It is a corner-café-cum-eatery-cum-shop, and it's simply wonderful. You will have some of the happiest memories of your lives if you go, stop and eat there – outside if possible, in good weather. There is fish, fish, and lots more fish, all as fresh as can be, and all having as little as possible done to them. My phone has been red-hot for two years now with all kinds of people phoning me to tell me they have 'discovered' Fishy Fish Café. I've already been there, I crow.

A chance meeting with Michelin-starred Robbie Millar in Marks and Spencer seemed like a good occasion to tell him about it, but he just blurted out: 'That's the place that Paul [Rankin] was telling me about! He stopped in mid-mouthful of hake to phone and tell me all about it, such was his excitement.' It became apparent as the tale went on and details were swapped that myself and The Rankin had had an equally superb experience there. When next I met Paul at lunch in his Belfast eatery Cayenne, I mentioned Robbie, the phone call, the café, and the food tale. He stopped, stooped, and intoned: 'Éamonn, there should be one of those Fishy Fish places at every street corner of every town in Ireland!' So now. Ye've been telt.

Ah, Cork! Where else would you be going? As befits the biggest county in Ireland – and, moreover, the biggest foodie county – no less an august publication than *Gault et Millau* devoted an entire issue to west Cork some years back: the first time that the magazine had ever entertained anywhere outside France. These days, everyone beats a trail to the county, for there is a wealth of places that should be visited and indulged in. It is far beyond the scope of this book to name them all; all I can do is list a few favourites. In addition to the establishments mentioned, do seek out the wonderful cheese Milleens. You must also try the aforementioned black pudding from Clonakilty, which is justly

186

famous. And go to Michel Philipott's Ty ar Mor in Skibbereen for some of the finest Breton cuisine outside Brittany. Oh, and while you're there, pop upstairs for, unbelievably, the best Thai cooking I have had anywhere in Ireland. That's Cork for you.

*

No one can deny the amazing progress that has been made in the restaurant sector in relation to Irish food over the past number of years. While London may still claim to be the gastronomic capital of Europe (though Lyon may well dispute this), some of the world's most exciting food is to be found in Ireland.

Just how much of this is 'Irish' food, however? Ireland, like Britain a nation arguably without a true culinary history, is a sponge for the world's cuisines and wines. In France, non-French wines are a rarity – and an expensive one at that – and one would be hard-pushed to find a fine Bordeaux in Italy. And why not? Why would one wine-producing country import wine from another? In Ireland, by contrast, our shelves are stocked with the world's wines – and this is not always the good thing that it seems. The wines of Australia, as popular as they are, are not always conducive to food. Made by a largely Anglo-Saxon population for drinking rather than accompanying food, they often lack subtlety and restraint and can be very heavy.

This same mix-and-match approach is to be found in many restaurants, where some chefs seem to think that the more eccentric the combination on the plate, the more modern, innovative or trendy the result. Sadly, the finished dish is not always the sum of its parts, and certainly will not stand the test of time.

This magpie cuisine often rings hollow. One of the problems in modern-day Ireland is that, while the restaurant experience has improved out of all recognition, the domestic situation has not followed suit, with many people still unaware of what a balanced meal is: one that offers taste and harmony and is prepared with flair. Thus, in a restaurant we are often titillated by the flash and the novel – until the 'next big thing' comes along.

It could be argued that the 'French' cuisine offered in many of Ireland's French restaurants can only be truly French if the produce comes from France. Generally, these restaurants are using Irish produce in a French manner. There is nothing in itself wrong with this, but the customer will rarely be offered a Limousin piece of beef, as in France – even if the sauce is judged correctly! In the absence of a true Irish cuisine, the closest we can come to achieving such a cuisine is by using the best and freshest Irish ingredients exclusively. Since there is nothing new under the sun, the result may be judged to be Irish, even though the recipe may contain such modern constituents as sun-dried tomatoes, lemongrass or pasta.

In that spirit, here is a personal recipe – based on classic French techniques – that shows off some truly native ingredients.

A *pissaladière* is a tart closely related to pizza that is native to the city of Nice. The difference is that it is made with shortcrust pastry. The *pissaladière* is very simple – it consists of tomatoes, olives, anchovies and onions – and is meant to be eaten in slices. I rework the idea here and present it in a restaurant-style fashion.

for the pastry:
200g flour
125g Irish butter
Sea salt
1 egg
Water, to bind

for the sauce:
6 ripe tomatoes, seeded and chopped
1 large onion
Bay leaf, fresh thyme, salt and pepper

for the topping:
1 Clonakilty black pudding
1 Irish goat's cheese (such as St Tola)

Make the pastry as for Alsace onion tart (page 171). Then gently fry the onions in a little olive oil with the bay leaf and thyme until softened, then add the peeled and roughly chopped tomatoes, salt and pepper. If neccessary, add a little tomato purée to thicken and lengthen the sauce.

Roll out the pastry to a thin circle and fit it into the mould. Spread the onion-and-tomato sauce around the circumference of the pastry circle. Arrange slices of black pudding on top, interspersed with broken pieces of goat's cheese. Place in a hot oven for twelve to eighteen minutes and serve. Try it with a green salad and washed down with a glass of Curim beer from Carlow!

KERRY

I first visited the Kingdom of Kerry in 1958 or 1959, travelling by train all the way from Belfast – a thrilling journey for a young boy fascinated by railways. I remember the tram lines still in O'Connell Street, the loop line over Dublin and, most of all, the trains driving right into the wall at Westland Row, as it seemed to me.

Limerick Junction, with its criss-cross network of lines, was a heart-stopping sight for a four-year-old budding anorak, and Killarney long ago was a railway near-paradise for a wee boy with two whole weeks to spend exploring. Happily, the food was just like at home: the Cornflakes were exactly the same and milk flowed freely from a bottle and had never been near a cow.

I didn't return to Kerry for years. When I eventually did, it was not specifically to find the best restaurants or to admire the beautiful scenery – though both exist in abundance – but rather to discover a single and unique product, a superb meat that was revered by those in the know and had yet to be discovered by myself.

The great Irish writer Mairtín Ó Cadháin once said that, in dealing with and writing in Irish, he felt 'two thousand years old'. Similar thoughts occurred to me as I circumnavigated a gloriously sunny Dingle peninsula, looking for the boat that would take me over to the ancient rock of the Great Blasket Island. Since 1953, the island has been barren save for some ruins, a varied flora and fauna, and numerous sheep, although its legacy of literature, and its remote and tranquil setting, guarantees it a steady stream of visitors. I was spellbound by this isolated, craggy lump, this former cradle of the Irish language that had spawned so many writers and storytellers, and was now willing me to come over.

It was a hot, clear day like few in Ireland. The trip across on the Peig Sayers ferry was thrilling, the backdrop of the Kerry mainland sheer, and the anticipation of setting foot on the most westerly point in Europe at once overwhelming and becalming. I leave it to greater writers than myself to describe the magnificence of the maritime wilderness: my job was to find out about the afor-mentioned sheep, the Blasket Island lamb.

Shortly after arriving on the deserted island, I found myself in the presence of two men, Donncha and Seamas – real men, sur-rounded by their four dogs, great staffs in hand, tending their sheep with care as they do year after year. For a brief moment, I felt that a city slicker like myself could be persuaded to give it all up and join them, free on the slopes of the Great Blasket, two thousand years old, unflinching in the briny breeze, living off the fruit of my labours. Then I remembered, of course, that these were real men and I wasn't, and the moment was gone.

Donncha Ó Ceileachar explained to me that storytelling, place names and traditional song show that the Blasket lamb has surely been reared on the island for a very long time. In addition, the island's famous writings of the twentieth century not only men-tioned the importance of lambing to the economy of the islanders but also referred to the demand among the butchers of Dingle for this most succulent of lamb.

When the islanders abandoned the Great Blasket in the fifties and sixties, the lambing more or less ceased, however. When sheep-farming began once more on the island in the eighties, it was initially the abattoirs that took the lambs in, though they made no distinction between meat from the islands and meat from any-where else. Fortunately, a change occurred in the nineties, when it became clear that people were beginning to show more interest in the foods they eat and how those products come to be. In par-ticular, organic methods were in vogue; subsequently, demand for organic meats, and specifically Blasket Island lamb, increased.

The lambs are reared on the island with the sea all around: they are free to wander and to graze at will. It would simply not be possible to conceive of a more organic and natural setting, the air heavy with salt, and grass and naturally growing herbs in abun-dance. The magnificent meat that results from this is available from one butcher in Dingle, Gerry Kennedy. Visitors to the area who have enjoyed it so much in the many fine restaurants dotted around Kerry seek it out, and Gerry is no stranger to sending it up to Cork and Dublin. As is so often the case with such products, demand far outstrips supply.

The season for this lamb lasts from mid-July to September, and only around a hundred and twenty or a hundred and thirty lambs are reared. Getting them from the Great Blasket to the mainland is not difficult, but great care is taken in doing so. In effect, the lambs are transferred to an intermediate island on their way to the mainland so as not to upset them unduly. This smaller island is called An Fear Marbh, so called becase it resembles a dead man lying in the middle of the sea. After they have rested and relaxed once more, they are ferried over the last stretch of water to the mainland.

Depsite all this information, I had little inkling of what exactly I was dealing with when I came to cook Great Blasket lamb for the first time. I cooked it as I would any other leg of lamb, and noted its hearty red colour and fine smell. When I finally removed it from the oven and allowed it to rest for some ten minutes before carving it for plating, I became aware that I was dealing with something quite different, however.

In the first place, preparing it as I had in the Breton manner, it struck me that the French would kill for lamb such as this. Lamb is rightly esteemed in France and the French revere their own *agneau pre-sale* above any other. Imagine if they knew about this, a natural lamb constantly marinated live in the salt air!

When I carved into the centre of the lamb for the first time, the cooked-just-so flesh is revealed, succulent and deep-red like a fine Burgundy – the colour matching that of my deeply sunburnt face! At this stage, it became apparent that the texture of the meat was quite different from that of any common-or-garden lamb. Thick and chunky, yet soft, it oozed juices copiously; as I carved through the flesh, it was difficult to resist grabbing a slice and beginning to eat.

When I came to taste it, I understood just what it is that sets this lamb apart: the magnificent hint of sea salt in the bite as pleasure is taken in the chewing, and the gradual delicacy of flavour that emerges before swallowing, underpinned by an innate and robust herbiness. Did it need those slivers of garlic with which I stabbed it before roasting, since the flavour is of itself so outspoken and so multifaceted that it scarcely needs any enhancement?

I thought of the Italians and their admirable practice of inserting anchovies into a leg of lamb such as this before cooking *abbachio alla Romana*. Such an addition would be totally redundant here: in the first place, there is no lamb such as this, and in the second place that elusive salty tang is already there naturally.

In the end, I would urge that nothing, except for a little seasoning on the outside, be added to the cut. By all means serve roast garlic along with it, but not in it. Herb the sauce or accompanying potatoes or other starch, but leave the lamb unadorned, the better to savour it.

Blasket Island lamb is one of Ireland's great gastronomic treasures: it deserves an *appellation contrôlée,* a badge of recognition like the one that adorns every *poulet de Bresse* from Burgundy. Most of all, you owe it to yourself to try it at least once. Two recipes for preparing it are given below, and details of some fine Kerry tables where you might enjoy it are given in the directory at the end of the book.

Roast Blasket Island lamb
with a Cashel Blue, walnut and chive butter

Blasket Island lamb is so beautiful that it needs little accompaniment save a few pan juices and fresh herbs. As I have writtten above, cooking and tasting this exquisite meat was such a revelation that I regretted some of the things that I did to it, such as inserting slivers of garlic – something I would always do to a roast leg of lamb – but that are simply not necessary in this instance.

So I have thought long and hard about the best way to cook the lamb. It occurs to me that the following approach might be appropriate.

1 leg of Blasket Island lamb
1 glass white wine
454g (one large packet) Irish butter
75g mature Cashel Blue cheese
25g walnuts
Bunch of chives, finely chopped
Peanut oil or olive oil
12 cloves of garlic
1 bag of young spinach
1kg potatoes, boiled and mashed
Bunch of fresh parsley
Fresh rosemary
Salt and black pepper
Bay leaves
1 egg

Heat some oil in a pan and add a little of the butter to it. Then add the leg to that, browning it all over. Season lightly with salt and to your taste with pepper. Cover generously with rosemary and bay leaves and place in an oven preheated to 180°C.

Then make the Cashel Blue butter. Loosen 400g of the butter with the back of a fork, then finely crumble the cheese into it and add the chives. Chop the walnuts roughly and incorporate them into the butter mixture. Combine all the ingredients thoroughly, then spoon the mixture onto a sheet of aluminium foil and fashion the butter into the shape of a sausage. Wrap the foil around the butter, twist each end like a Christmas cracker and place in the freezer.

Put the cloves of garlic, still in their skins, into a pot of boiling water. After about five minutes, remove the cloves but keep the water for the spinach.

The potatoes should be mashed very well so that there are no lumps. Add the egg to the potatoes, then a drizzle of olive oil, salt and pepper. Combine all these ingredients and keep warm.

The leg of lamb should be roasted pink after about firty-five minutes, or longer if you want it cooked more. About ten minutes before it is ready, place the blanched garlic cloves around the lamb. When the meat is ready, remove it from the oven and leave to one side for fifteen minutes before carving.

Return the pan to the heat and add the wine to the pan juices with a little butter. Swirl over the flame to form a simple herb-flavoured sauce. Strain and reserve. Blanch, drain and season the spinach.

Carve the lamb. Place some of the mash on the plate, put the spinach on top, and finally the lamb. Drizzle a little of the sauce around this. Place three of the garlic cloves around the edge of the plate.

Remove the butter from the freezer, slice, and place as much as desired on the lamb slices. Finally, place two or three whole chives attractively on the meat. Then get stuck in!

LIMERICK

We have to get one thing straight from the start: this chapter is not entitled 'In Praise of Packet and Tripe'. In case you're wondering, packet and tripe is Limerick's delicacy. This dish – tripe and blood sausage, the latter made with sheep's blood – is a traditional food that has been enjoyed in the city since the dawn of thyme and eaten by various GAA all-stars and rugby types, who still swear by it. They can have it. I confess that I didn't like it when I tasted it, and I can name others who didn't too! I will continue to eat *Tripes à la mode de Caen* when in Calvados and *tablier de sapeur* ('sapper's apron' – now there's a good name for a reel) when in Lyon, or even tripe as dim sum when in the Good World Chinese Restaurant in South Great George's Street in Dublin. But packet and tripe? Sorry.

'Limerick, you're a lay-by', as the parody of the old hit single goes. For many years, smug Dublin jackeens dismissed Limerick as a place *not* to go to. Indeed, I was surprised when one of Ireland's leading sommeliers, Alain Bras, left his employ in Whites on the Green in Dublin and went to set up home there and open Restaurant de la Fontaine in Gerald Griffin Street.

The first time I went to Limerick was to eat with him there (to give him a turn, as we used to say). At that time, the city seemed, well, a trifle grim, unwelcoming – and in stark contrast to the 'give it a lash' mentality of other Irish cities on the western seaboard. If Alain's restaurant was open for business at all, the good folk of 1980s Limerick didn't seem to pay it any mind. The restaurant was well ahead of its time: unsurprisingly, it has long since closed down.

Happily, things have changed: in the noughties, you can hardly get a table in Limerick, even at lunchtime. The much brighter pedestrianised city centre, which still has its strange grid-like pattern of streets, is breezy and cheerful, spotted with restaurants – and buzzing.

Since that first visit, I've walked those streets many a time. There is of course the usual coterie of Indian and Chinese restaurants and takeaways, though one of them, the Yellow Lemon, gets full marks not just for being a Tandoori restaurant with an original name but also for a having an all-encompassing website *(www.theyellowlemon.com)*, which is full of information, and deatails of specials and offers.

Lately, I have been able to eschew the Indian and Chinese establishments – though this is not to denigrate the many fine Asian restaurants that have opened in the last ten years. In the auld Ireland of recent memory, arriving in a strange town or city meant dining out in the first Chinese you came across, such was the dearth of decent places. A Chinese restaurant could either be a welcome surprise or, more often than not, an indifferent dining experience.

I was able to go out and try plenty of different establishments in Limerick. 'Try' is the apposite verb, for in recent years I have been denied a table in many of Limerick's better city-centre restaurants, such is the level of business they enjoy. Harrumph. Indignant, I tried desperately to get Terry Wogan's phone number, the rationale being: he's a son of Limerick, he'll know how to get a table. But he, hosting a lunchtime British TV show, was simply not available.

Fortunately, Bill Whelan, the city's foremost composer, was available, and he kindly gave me several addresses to try. Unfortunately, all of the places he recommended were full: this only served to lead me a merry riverdance (ouch) around the city. But in so doing, I discovered little basement places like the Piccola Italia in O'Connell Street and the excellent and inviting Tiger Lily's, grand of design and thrilling of food. The lesson is: book – and arrive – early.

Of all of these new restaurants, none has pleased me more than Brûlées, on Upper Henry Street. As the name suggests, this establishment serves one of the finest crème brûlées in the jurisdiction. Much more than this, it provides magnificent lunches and dinners, grandiose but sensible portions, sure-footed cooking, and minimalist prices. Brûlées is run by Belfastman Donal Cooper and his Galwegian partner Teresa Murphy, who is also the head chef. The pair established the restaurant in May 1998, having met at the catering college in Portrush, County Antrim.

Lunch should not be missed, not just for the sheer value it offers but also because it presents a harmonious marriage of flavours and tastes – modern Mediterranean cuisine with an Irish twist. Not surprisingly, Brûlées has become extremely popular with 'foodies' from all over the country. They are no doubt attracted by the home-made breads served daily with the finest of Greek olives and hummus, as a prelude to other delights.

The menu oozes modern Irish culinary confidence: starters include Skellig crab claws cooked in butter, garlic and Old Bay seasoning (a blend of celery, onion and spices), classic Caesar salad of romaine lettuce with garlic croutons, Caesar dressing and Parmigiano Reggiano – note the absence in this dish of such blow-ins as 'char-grilled chicken' and the like – and cherry tomato, buffalo mozzarella, pine-nut and basil tartlet, drizzled with truffle oil. Simple and to the point.

There is a particular emphasis on fresh fish, and it is here that the menu really gets going: black sole, turbot, sea bass and John Dory are frequently on offer as 'fish of the day'. And even a jaded palate like mine, tired of so-so, overcooked salmon, could get very excited about fresh fillet of salmon with crabmeat and king prawns, cooked in a creamy corn, tomato and saffron chowder. The specials, such as oriental crispy duck or corn-fed chicken, should also be tried. There are of course steaks a-plenty, but for an alternative to fish, I would have my old favourite, supreme of guinea fowl. Presented as it is here, stuffed with Brie, bacon and herbs, and accompanied by asparagus, with a simple warm dressing of soy and truffle oil, it sounds too good to resist.

Donal and Teresa appreciate the importance of offering the freshest and best produce: they support small suppliers where possible. The result shows on the plate, and their continued success is guaranteed. Next time you're there, wave: that's me over in the corner table.

Another oasis of civilisation in Limerick is Paddy O'Flynn's Devine Wines boutique. (At least it was 'Devine Wines' when I was last there, but it has been such a success that outlets have been opening all over Munster, and a name-change, to 'The Wine Buff', has ensued.) Here is a wine shop that has filled a gap in the market. In director Paddy's words, the Irish market was tiring of commercial, mass-produced wines. After a meeting with a sympathetic Irish bank manager in Paddy's premises in Bordeaux, where he lives most of the year, Paddy was easily persuaded to open a new shop in Limerick, which has thrived. There are now no fewer than five Wine Buff shops throughout Munster.

It is a boutique that has a simple elegance and a warm glow – though my memory of the latter may be down to the excellent wines that I sampled there rather than the decor. The wines are fine, the prices keen – after all, their slogan is 'extraordinary wines at ordinary prices' – but, above all, it is a place of great conviviality where, before you purchase, you can sample wines in the company of enthusiasts who will extol, proselytise – and have a drink with you.

The Wine Buff is an outstanding shop and I hope that their current franchise policy will soon extend over the country as a whole. Although that happy eventuality would bring magnificent wines within reach of all for a reasonable outlay, the location of the Limerick shop in Mallow Street means that it is but a hop and a step (we'll forget the jump) from Brûlées, where – oh joy – many of the Wine Buff's wines are on offer in a stunning example of the least vicious circle on earth. How do you franchise that?

There are many fine crèmes brûlées to be eaten round this fair country of ours, and far too many in Cayenne for any sane man to recount. When, betimes, it's off the menu, one can always seek solace in their excellent buttermilk panna cotta, truly the finest expression in desserts of marrying a typical Irish ingredient to Italian style and panache.

I raise a glass too to the memory of what must have been Dublin's most sublime crème brûlée – that which was served in the now defunct and much-missed Moe's of Baggot Street. A hint, though: one can now find the chef from Moe's in Bruno's of Kildare Street, which should of course be renamed 'Crème Brûlée Street'.

My ageing tum means that I can no longer enjoy this dessert at night, as I now find it difficult to digest. I am forced, therefore, *forced*, to have them only at lunchtime. I can think of no better example, nor no finer to place to go for a lunchtime treat of one, than Brûlée's of Limerick, whose spot-on recipe for this temptress of a dessert, raspberry tuiles forbye, is here presented with lust. Not love, lust.

for the brûlée:
5 large egg yolks
Half-litre cream
1 vanilla pod
1 small dessertspoon cornflour
5 dessertspoons caster sugar

for the tuiles:
225g fresh raspberries
2 tablespoons soft butter
Half a cup of icing sugar
2 tablespoons flour

Serves 4

Mix the yolks, sugar and cornflour. Split and scrape the vanilla pod, add to the cream and bring to the boil. When the cream is boiled, add all to the egg mix. Whisk well and place on a bain-marie; stir constantly until the mixture thickens. Leave to infuse for fifteen minutes. Strain, pour into ramekins, and allow to set. When serving, sprinkle with brown sugar and, with the use of a blowtorch, heat the sugar until it melts and forms a caramel top. Serve immediately.

Purée the raspberries and strain through a fine mesh strainer. Reserve three tablespoons of the purée. Blend the sugar and butter with a wooden spoon, add the purée and mix well. Add the flour and mix until smooth. Cover the mixture with clingfilm and rest in the fridge for one hour. Make a template from a plastic top from, say, a yogurt or ice-cream container by cutting out a circle about 6cm in diameter, leaving the rim intact. Smooth out a small teaspoon of the mixture into the centre of the template with a spatula. Bake in small batches, say two or three at a time, in an oven preheated to 150°C, for eight to ten minutes, or until the tuiles are lacy and very lightly browned; they burn easily, so do not leave the kitchen! Allow to cool on the baking sheet, then store in an airtight container.

CLARE

The more I write about the counties of Ireland, the more I am reminded that long before I began to trawl those counties for the food that I enjoy so much today, music was my connection to them: the jigs, reels, polkas and slides of Ireland.

Many's the *fleadh cheoil* that were attended, wet fields slept in, long nights spent in pubs in the 1970s attempting to explain to French friends why there was 'nothing to eat in Ireland'. God be with the days when as a long-haired hippy I began to cultivate the self-image of an upmarket republican, my Armagnac in one hand and a bouzouki in the other.

Of all the counties of Ireland, none was more familiar to me than Clare, by virtue of its regal music – and its mythical person-ages, such as Mrs Crotty and her reel from *The Chieftains 2* or Willy Clancy, the master piper, who would have swapped his skill on the pipes overnight for the 'sweet music of the Irish language'. Then there was Junior Crehan, the tin-whistle player, whose 'favourite' reel was made famous on the very first classic 'black' Planxty album.

'Junior' was made flesh to me at the Inter-celtic Festival in Lorient – an excuse for an orgy of great music, drink and late-night food down at the Port de Pêche – where he brought atten-tion to my legendary absent-mindedness with the timeless 'Ara, you'd lose your bollocks only they're in a bag, and you'd lose that only it's tied on to you.'

But despite all these musical ties to Clare, it was the one coun-ty in Ireland that I had never managed to visit, until the beginning of the twenty-first century. It became very easy to get to, as Aer Lingus had provided a marvellous link from Belfast to Shannon whereby one could get cheaply to the 'wesht' in just forty-five minutes; unfortunately, in the wake of the September 11 atrocity, that has now gone.

In 2000, having been invited to attend a recording in a local studio, I duly made my way to County Clare on the big Airbus. I remember instantly liking the feel of Ennis as I alighted from the connecting bus from Shannon Airport. As usual, I was beginning to wonder (for 'wonder', read 'worry') where a chap might get something to eat, when I stopped into an unlikely-looking deli in a narrow side street. The deli had a great variety of foods on offer: no sooner had I asked for a cheese-and-ham sandwich than I was challenged as to whether I wanted Emmenthal, Gruyère or Comte, Jamon de Serrano, Bayonne or Parma?

I couldn't believe it: that was the day that I stopped in my tracks and marvelled at just how much Ireland had changed and how quality grub could be found in the very first premises that I entered – unlike in my native Belfast. I resisted phoning those moaning French friends, François, Dede and Fredo, to show off how the new gourmet Ireland was here and had moved on so decisively from the ubiquitous Easy Singles. 'Tain't nice to crow.

The experience also set me to thinking about how much cheese had become part of the fabric of Irish life – and about the many varieties and artisan products that were now available. Oh, I admit I'd pooh-poohed the early Irish cheeses when they first appeared, way back when. One was Camembert-like but tasteless, and more expensive than the French model it sought to emulate; it also had a *pâte molle* ('soft skin') like Rizla cigarette papers. But from those early days back in the 1980s a whole new industry had grown up, bringing us names that many of us now wondered at a distance how to pronounce – like Durrus or Cooleeney or especially Mine Ghabhair – unfathomable for some but exquisite for all.

It was a time of successes with the likes of Cork's Milleens taking a gold medal in Paris, ahead of well-established French cheeses. But it was also a time of problems, with the powers-that-be taking a dim view of unpasteurised raw-milk products and imposing, no doubt with good intentions, strict readings of EU law, resulting in many tasteless and therefore pointless appellations, and taking us back to the bad old days of Cheddar. (I have to confess here to a long hatred of Cheddar. Hanging's too good for it, and in my opinion it represents an offence against the state. Would that the EU would ban it. Or better still, have it repackaged, as befits it, as soap.)

Thus it was that, for a long time, Irish cheese was composed solely of derivatives – the Camembert-like, the Cheddar-like and the Gruyère-like – you can even get a Tipperary Emmenthal. Eventually, even a blue cheese worthy of the name came on the market – Cashel Blue, joined by another, St Crozier.

There was one essential type of cheese, however, that was still to be found wanting: a decent chèvre or goat's cheese. But finally, the name 'St Tola' (the Irish adopting the French habit of naming cheeses after saints) forced itself on my gastro-conciousness. I believe the first time I saw it was on a menu somewhere in the guise of a St Tola mash served with Irish beef.

The dish intrigued me, and via the proof of the pudding – which was delicious – I resolved to find out more about this exquisite and creamy but tangy Irish goat's cheese from Clare. I didn't have to try very hard, for around this time the new producer of the cheese, Siobhan Ní Ghairbhith, was writing to head chefs the length and breadth of the land, myself included. It didn't take long to get from the twang of the banjo to the tang of St Tola – though appalling jokes like that kept me in the day job for decades.

This remarkable Irish cheese is made in the townland of Inagh, just south of the Burren. For more than twenty years it has been produced here by Meg and Derrick Gordon, though in 1999 that responsibility was taken over by their neighbour Siobhan.

These days visitors to the farm and to the state-of-the-art cheese rooms are encouraged: I think it's the first time that I have ever gone a-gambolling in the fields with the sources of my foodstuffs, when I too dropped in a few years back (though in the course of making TV food programmes this was to become an exercise that was oft-repeated, most notably with some ostriches).

My new-found fellow gambollers were the Toggenburg and Saanen goats who make up the St Tola herd. The herd includes a hundred and twenty milking goats, thirty kids and fair pucks. Kidding starts on the farm in early February and continues until mid-May. Every year the herd increases by keeping the offspring from the best milkers. The sixty-five-acre organic farm provides the goats with rich grass and hay; they are also fed organic grains.

The cheese range now comprises several varieties: there are the classic St Tola logs and crottins, ideal for cooking and using in warm salads. These cheeses grill well, preferably under a salamander or a domestic mounted grill, where the heat comes down from above, though the crottins can take heat directly on a grill-pan, which leaves the cheese seared with attractive black indentations. While cooking intensifies the flavour, just chomping on a slice with a lump of fresh, crispy baguette and lots of red wine to quaff is one of life's great pleasures, enhanced when you have the Cliffs of Moher in full view. Nowadays there is also a hard cheese, a feta, and a diced St Tola cheese in oil.

The indefatigable Siobhan points out that the whole operation is organic and that the cheeses are made by hand, seven days a week. Following her recent spell in France learning new techniques, the St Tola range is metamorphosing into a finer and more mature cheese as the market develops and Irish people demand a more flavoursome fermented curd. *Treise leat, a Shiobhain!*

The name of this dish means 'the silkweaver's brain'. The silk-weavers were an all-important part of Lyon's population and economy; 'cervelle' is a reference to the appearance of the dish (which is also called 'claquaret' because the cheese, which should be 'male', or firm, has been well-beaten, or claqué). Every restaurant makes their own version of this cheese, with fromage blanc, shallots, parsley, chervil, chives, white wine, white-wine vinegar, and sometimes pink peppercorns. They serve it between the main course and dessert without so much as a by-your-leave.

400g of fromage blanc
60g of shallots, peeled and chopped
1 clove of garlic, crushed smooth
150g of thick crème fraiche
1 tablspoon of red-wine vinegar
1 glass of dry white wine
1 bunch of chives, finely chopped
A generous pinch of pink peppercorns
1 tablespoon of good olive or peanut oil
Salt and pepper

Serves 4

Mix the fromage blanc in a large salad bowl with the shallots, garlic, chives, crème fraiche, vinegar, wine, oil, salt and pepper. Beat everything together thoroughly. Keep in the fridge for a couple of hours before use. That's it.

Serve chilled, with the pink peppercorns sprinkled on top, and eat with a fresh, crisp baguette. The famous Lyonnais chef Paul Bocuse adds parsley, tarragon and chervil to the dish, as well as the chives; he also beats in the vinegar to the fromage blanc before adding the oil.

There are great clams – and lobsters – to be had in Newquay, County Clare. I've been about a bit but I've never seen clams as fresh, as alive, as impressive as these buckos. They scurried about all over the place – despite the fact that they have no legs!

Naturally I had to eat them, but I was in two minds as to what to do with them. Eat 'em fresh with a *sauce mignonette* (see recipe on page 88)? Or cooked in the classic Italian manner, as *spaghettini alle vongole*? I opted for the latter, as I had no knife with me to open them. Strangely enough, though, I did have a box of Barilla *spaghettini* (*numero uno* in Italia!) in my back pocket. As you do.

1 packet of *spaghettini* (Traditonally, spaghetti is used in this dish, but I prefer this thinner variety. Then again, that's breaking the cardinal rule of not messing with Italian cooking. So sue me!)
1.5kg of clams
Olive oil
Plenty of freshly chopped parsley
Salt and pepper

Bring a large pot of water with a little salt in it to the boil. Add the *spaghettini* and stir it in with a two-pronged fork. Leave it to cook for around four to five minutes. (The instructions on the box may instruct you to cook it for far too long: instead, taste it regularly and drain when it is still a little underdone, as it will be cooked a little more with the clams.) Return it to the pot with some of the cooking water. While the *spaghettini* is cooking, place all the clams in a wide-bottomed frying pan over a fairly high heat and add a little olive oil. After a while, the clams will begin to open and release their juices. When they have all opened, toss the cooked *spaghettini* with its cooking water into them, throw in the parsley and mix throughly. Season with salt and pepper to taste. The pasta will now be perfectly al dente. Don't even think of adding or using Parmesan, or you will be arrested and imprisoned by the Italian food police!

CONNACHT

GALWAY

*Dra*í*ocht,* that's the word. I believe that there's a permanent magic in the air in Galway. It dances up Quay Street and Shop Street, hangs on every jig, on every reel, and even on the odd hornpipe from the many musicians dotted around the city, and creates a great impression on native, blow-in and visitor alike. Galway is a city like none other in Ireland: it parties, and it parties hard. It is the gateway to Connemara, beloved of Continental visitors, who have long been drawn here, not just by the mythical landscape – that beauty of the barren, that reality of the no-longer-hidden Ireland on your camera lens – but also by such naff Continental hits celebrating the place as Sardou's *'Les Lacs du Connemara',* once hijacked by Fianna Fáil and Squire Haughey for an election campaign.

The towns, countryside and restaurants of County Galway are also well known to food-lovers. These places and their excellent produce – seafood of course being paramount – have been described at length in other publications. I am here concerned with the city of Galway, though I will make especial mention of one fine establishment in the prim village of Oughterard.

Le Blason, slap in the middle of the village, is run by Daniel and Marie Cuel. This restaurant, a classical-French establishment, is crouched next to the River Corrib and has a beautiful down-stairs dining room. Daniel, the chef-patron, looks for all the world like a French chef of the old school, all whites and ample belly, with the clichéd generous moustache to match. He came to Ireland after falling in love with Connemara following some fishing trips there in the late 1960s and is now in semi-retirement.

You would be forgiven for thinking that he would champion his native Breton or French cuisine alone, but in fact Daniel has travelled the world and cooked and lived in countries as disparate as Japan, Thailand, Russia, Vietnam and the French West Indies. While his day-to-day menu is both tempting and above reproach, Daniel is thus in a unique position to offer dining experiences from all of the countries mentioned above – and often does, to parties of six or more. As a result, in as unlikely a setting as a small west-of-Ireland village, you can experience a full Japanese meal in all its glory. (I'm up for the full Vietnamese treatment, a personal favourite. Anybody who wants to make up a six-some, get in touch!)

One very special item on his menu is *cari gost,* an unusual product of his home town of Lorient. The town was once a gateway for trading ships to the East; at that time, its name was spelled 'L'orient': 'the East'. Since those days, the *département* of Morbihan, of which Lorient is the chief town, has been allowed by law to sell *cari gost,* a unique blend of Asian spices that is available only in pharmacies there – and in no other French *département.* Close in nature to the North African spice mix known as *ras-al-hanout* or an Indian curry mix ('cari', from the Tamil word 'kari', is the correct way to spell 'curry' in French), it is an invigorating blend of heady spices that is indispensable with seafood, especially shellfish. Daniel makes sure that his daughter keeps him regularly supplied with the mixture, which he uses to work wonders on his majestic fresh fish.

In fact, if you go to Le Blason, try his brilliant interpretation of *lotte à l'Armoricaine* ('monkfish, in the Breton style'), and if you can give him some notice, he may prepare for you the wonderful fish-soup-cum-sublime-dish from Lorient known as *la cotriade,* the Breton version of bouillabaisse. Although *la cotriade* is generally best eaten at the Port de Pêche in Lorient, this delightful setting by the Corrib will do just as well.

But back to Galway city. I have to admit, I love going there. The magic begins as soon as the *Cú na Mara* train hits Athenry (though I don't recommend spending any time there: it can be very lonely in the fields that immediately surround Athenry). Galway is a wonderful place to stroll in, in all weathers. Of course, I'm not pretending that it is idyllic in winter, when it can be ruddy freezing, but that's when the magic kicks in: even in the depths of January, in the middle of a fog that London would envy, the spirit of the city is irrepressible. Walk down by the Claddagh on a dark evening and listen to the water roar to the sea: that's the sound of *draíocht.*

The city is dotted with little places where you can have a snack or just take coffee, and there are all manner of wine bars, brasseries, cheap 'n' cheerful hideouts, great Indian, Thai and Chinese restaurants, and loads of fun little bistros. The one thing that Galway hasn't taken to too well is the upmarket restaurant – perhaps because the natives perceive them to be pretentious.

This attitude to pretentiousness suits the city: Galway has always had a laid-back, devil-may-care attitude, which I adore. For long a home of itinerant musicians, Breton *refoulés* (those avoiding their military service) and assorted new-agers, its devotion to bonhomie, and to bohemia, is famous. Be careful: you could easily stay a few days here and never leave. Mind you, sometimes the magic gets to me so much that I feel I possibly overrate the place: some of the food establishments could certainly be judged as being on the wrong side of studenty. (Galway is, of course, a university town.) For a long time, Galway was a pints-and-music city – a place of immense craic, best experienced in pubs that these days are no longer quite so smoky. But the city, perhaps due to its large intake of Bretons and French expats, took to Ireland's burgeoning food renaissance with gusto, and in the early days of that revolution its atmosphere was different from that of other towns in Ireland by virtue of the little bakeries, offering home-made baguettes, and crêperies dotted round its close-knit streets.

The city's never-ending influx of people from far-flung places is paying off. The Galway market on Saturday mornings is now justly famous – and one of the city's most colourful events – a genuine treat for food-lovers. Arriving there at what I believed to be the ungodly hour of 8 AM, I was told I was already too late for the best of the morning's wares. The bustling market was a carnival of flavours and tastes: one could wander from organic-vegetable stalls run by Irish enthusiast growers to others selling all manner of the most exotic and varied foodstuffs and tended by swarthier types who were definitely not native to the county.

Here were colourful displays of olives of all sizes, visibly superb free-range eggs, dazzling white feta cheese marinated in oil and sundried tomatoes, a crêperie on wheels, and then the appetite-loosening odour of *chapatti* bread pockets with potato and other curries, reminding me of my beloved roadside *roti* shops (selling curries in flat Indian *roti* bread) in Trinidad.

213

Further along the row of stalls were to be found Moroccan flatbreads, hummus, tapenades, pastas, sauces and dips. All in all, it was the most fun shopping for food that I have had in years. It says a lot for Galwegians and the state of food in Galway today that so many of the locals had already visited the market at daybreak in order to snare the best of the produce.

At the top of the market is the busy emporium that is Sheridan's, full of cheeses, their salt tang strong on the palate when you taste them. A chap's knees could give way as he contemplated the mesmerising display of Irish and mainly French cheeses. For myself, I let out little yelps as I spotted my favourites, not the stuff of your average supermarket: Époisses, Vacheron and Comte. Here too are hams, salamis, prosciutto – all of the finest quality – and, to complete your day's shopping, an upstairs wine boutique, one of the country's finest. And I found myself insanely jealous, wishing that Belfast could be like this, where a meal could be put together in seconds following a simple trip down to the local market, brushing shoulders with fellow enthusiasts, the promise of a fine espresso to reward your efforts, nearby.

But look now at the crowded main drag of Shop Street and Quay Street; this is Gaillimh le Gaeilge, a knobbled, craggy, misshapen street. It is long and winding, and alive with music and colourful little shops, cafés and bistros. Oh, and you must try Nimmos at the Spanish Arch for great in-house music, an inexpensive wine list and great Continental fare, with keen prices.

Back up the street there are such weird and wonderful places as the Druid Lane restaurant and the marvellously named River God Café. At the Café du Journal, with its home-from-home atmosphere, you can rub shoulders with the great and good of the Irish-music world, sip one of the large range of European-style coffees on offer – and believe yourself to be in the centre of the known universe.

Further up the street is the antithesis of the older, smoke-stained eateries and cafés: the brand-new Ard Bia – a smashing name for a great little spot, all modern Moroccan pastels in a singularly clean, zingy and upbeat setting. Then, as dinner time approaches, it's back down the same street to the Quays Wine Bar and Restaurant, to dine in the friendliest of atmospheres – or, as I have done so often, just lounge and quaff Louis Roederer's fine entry-level brut – for stocking which, full marks to the Quays.

Quirky Galway is never too far away, with the likes of Banana-Phoblacht Café, a relaxed place run by Dutchman Alex Hijmans, who speaks fluent Ulster Irish and in his spare time writes some of the episodes for *Ros na Rún,* TG4's evening soap. It's true, I'm telling you. Indeed, not far from there are two excellent Indian restaurants, the Kashmir and the Bombay Palace. At these establishments, a chap can enjoy some truly first-class Indian cooking – and, if you are of that linguistic persuasion, be greeted and welcomed in Irish by Kumar, the most affable proprietor.

Such a list of Galway's finest is useful, but really, I must single out two establishments that stand out from the crowd. The first of these is Pierre's, in the middle of Quay Street, where simple but effective cuisine meets user-friendly prices head-on. In fact, Pierre's is a prime contender for Galway's leading restaurant of its type, and a paragon of excellence for the rest of the country to follow. First, though, I must declare a distant-but-slight interest, for working in the kitchen of this restaurant is a young Frenchman who also worked with me for many years in both Belfast and Dublin, and whose acquaintance I was delighted to make once more, quite by chance, on a recent visit to the City of the Tribes.

Behind every good chef, there's a great one, and Vincent Petit from Dunkirk is one of those master craftsmen, a true worker, an unashamed fan of food and drink, and someone who, through his many travels and experiences, is able to express his concept of good eating tirelessly, regularly and precisely. I know the quality of service that Vincent gave me as my sous-chef day after day, and I can truthfully say that I could not have done it without him, his uncanny ability to set up a kitchen in no time, and his anticipation of your needs, even at the most pressurised moments in a busy kitchen.

Now, Pierre's has benefited from his abilities, and I salute both him and his current chef, Roberto Basso, and marvel at what they have created between them in Galway: a restaurant that the city truly merits. Pierre's offers top-class, innovative cuisine, fixed-price menus, and a genuinely warm, friendly and, most important, informed and informative service. Go there, ask for

Vincent, mention my name, and reap the rewards.

The other restaurant which is a credit to the city is the relatively new Viña Mara, on the site of the old Brasserie 11. After my chance meeting with Vincent, he took me there with a 'Wait till ya see this' kind of look. When we arrived, a reception and raucous celebrations involving staff and management were in full swing to celebrate the winning of yet another award by Viña Mara's head chef, a young Mayoman by the name of Padraic Kielty.

I was intrigued: the restaurant looked beautiful, and the word on the floor that evening was that the young chef was quite brilliant. As I moved among the revellers, I met several of his former tutors and lecturers from catering college, all of whom were unanimous in their praise of this young lad. And it was 'just another award' for him in a long line of same: in the past five years, Padraic has represented Ireland all over the world, winning more than fifty medals. In 2003, at the International Culinary Championships, he won four gold medals – a record – and the overall award.

It was therefore a fairly humbling experience for me to meet this young man – who turned out to be probably the most modest and self-effacing chef I have ever met. Still, we managed to have a terrific chat about food and trends over a glass or several of champagne, which was flowing freely that everning. It turned out that I had enjoyed his cuisine several times in the past, as he had been the chef at Kirwan's Lane when it was the leading upmarket restaurant in the city.

Perhaps Viña Mara marks a turning point in Galway city's spiralling fortunes when it comes to food. For years, the county's finer establishments, such as Drimcong House and Ballynahinch Castle, have been scattered around the rest of the county, smug in their setting in the undisputed beauty of Connemara and sure of custom from jaded Continentals in search of unspoilt Ireland and its simpler way of life. But Viña Mara is unashamedly not a member of café-society Galway, or one of the latter-day hippy establishments or cute bistros. Instead, it's hip to the groove: a new and leading light of contemporary west-of-Ireland cooking. And in its young chef, Padraic Kielty, it has a trailblazer.

Lotte à l'armoricaine
– Monkfish, Breton style

This is a classic old-fashioned recipe that uses many staples of French cuisine, including butter, cream and cognac. The garnishes should be left fairly plain (to counterract the richness of the dish). I present the dish here in a more modern style. Certainly a monkfish tail would never be sliced in Brittany, but in this instance it will show off the precision of the cooking.

900g of monkfish tail
Glass Muscadet
Diced bacon
Tomato puree
Tomato *concassée* (diced)
White-wine vinegar
Glass of cognac
100ml cream
200ml fish stock
Olive oil
Cold unsalted butter, diced

Most of this dish can be cooked and finished in the frying pan. Remove any skin or membrane from the monkfish and fillet it. Place the frying pan over a high heat, add some olive oil, and when this begins to smoke, add the monkfish, sealing it all over and lightly colouring the outside. Reduce the heat, remove the monkfish and place it in the oven on a baking dish to cook, making sure that it remains a little moist in the middle. Then throw the diced bacon in to the pan. When this is thoroughly browned, add the Muscadet to the pan to deglaze, then add the fish stock and a dash of vinegar, increase the heat and leave to reduce.

When the sauce has reduced by a third, add the cream. When this has come to the boil, whisk in the cold diced butter and two tablespoons of olive oil. (The latter is far from traditional but adds a delightful and sympathetic flavour to sauces that goes particularly well with fish.) At this point, stir in a generous teaspoon of tomato purée to give a pale pink colour and a delicate flavour. Finally, add a dash of cognac.

Remove the monkfish from the oven, slice it and arrange it symmetrically on the plate. Pour the sauce around it and garnish with cold diced tomato in a corner of the plate. The dish could be served with rice, with new potatoes and baby white turnips, or with a fresh baguette.

STEAMED SCALLOPS WITH FENNEL AND LEEKS
WITH COCKLES-AND-MUSSELS GALETTES

One can find excellent crêpes and galettes in both parts of Britanny: the Pays Gallo (more French) and the Basse-Bretagne (more like the Breton equivalent of the Gaeltacht). A meal of galettes is usually eaten once a week in Breton households, either made by the housewife or bought in the local crêperie *(à emporter:* 'takeaway') at ridiculously low prices. If they are not eaten at home, then no self-respecting Breton would miss a visit to a crêperie once a week, where several *complêtes* (galettes with egg, ham and cheese) would be consumed, with a least one sweet crêpe to follow.

2 leeks
1 bulb of fennel
1 litre of water
16 scallops
3 carrots, peeled and coarsely chopped
1 stick of celery, coarsely chopped
2 cloves of garlic, peeled and crushed
200g cold butter, diced
Juice of half a lemon

for the galettes:
100g buckwheat flour
Water
Salt
3 eggs
Cockles and mussels

for the garnish:
Chives, chopped, and tomatoes, diced

Serves 4

Julienne the white part of the leek and coarsely chop the greens. Remove the base of the fennel and the three outer layers. Trim the tops and then slice the fennel into julienne strips. Keep these with the strips of leek. Roughly chop the rest of the bulb and put it with the leek greens, carrots, celery and garlic in the bottom part of the steamer. Add water, cover and boil for ten minutes.

Season the scallops generously with salt and pepper and put in the top part of the steamer. Arrange the julienned fennel and leek on top, then cover and steam for no more than ten minutes.

Put the butter and lemon juice in a small saucepan with a little water and boil very gently for three to four minutes until it is well blended and smooth. Taste and season the sauce before serving.

for the galettes:
Beat the eggs, season, and add the mussels and cockles. Keep this mixture to one side. Combine the buckwheat flour slowly with water and salt to obtain a fairly thick batter. Lightly oil a pan by dipping some kitchen roll in grapeseed or peanut oil and then wiping the base of the pan with it. Place the pan over a high heat, and when the oil begins to smoke add a ladleful of the galette batter. When this is cooked and detaches itself from the edges of the pan, flip it over. Add a generous amount of the mixture to the cooked side of the galette. When the egg is cooked to your taste, fold or roll the galette and serve.

to serve:
On a hot plate, serve the sauce first, then place the scallops with their leeks and fennel attractively on top. Place the galette to one side and garnish with the chives and tomatoes.

MAYO

I regret that my memories of Mayo will forever be tainted by my jaundiced vision of it. I was filthy, tired and battered by all the elements, soaked to the bone by a week of unceasing, uncaring rain, lying with one leg in the Mayo bog, the other possibly in a drier part of County Galway (though I won't swear to this), and attired in the same stinking clothes that I'd arrived in. It was a wet and completely food-free zone, and my misery was punctuated by nightly dreams of freedom, of Château Gruaud Larose, 'the wine of kings' and cherished favourite of Éamonn's, *sauce harissa,* unpasteurised Brie de Meaux, dinner at the Cherry Tree, Ar Vicoletto or Cayenne, a tagine of lamb with prunes, merguez sausages, a crusty baguette with apricot jam, and a steaming bowl of coffee as black as the Mayo night I now lay freezing in.

Why in God's name was this happening to me? Quite simply, because I'd taken a call from a TV company which, having lost Donncha Ó Dulaing of *Highways and Byways* fame, decided to ask me if I'd like to take part in their upcoming reality TV show, *S.O.S. (Seachtáin on Spotsholas:* 'A Week Out of the Spotlight'), to take place in the wilds of north Mayo.

And I, with typical lack of foresight – or what others call 'thought' – agreed, thinking it to be a cracking wheeze. I imagined the programme would involve walking, climbing, gliding and kayaking, that sort of thing, which I convinced myself I could do. Plus, it would keep my mug on the TV for another two months until the next series of *Bia's Bóthar.* But I overlooked one thing: I am utterly useless at most practical things, except maybe playing records, turning the TV on and charging mobile phones.

Everyone I knew thought it would be the best of craic and that almost certainly, once the cameras were turned off, we would spend the night in considerable luxury, only returning to our mocked-up tent, blue-mould bread and non-stop rain by day for the actual production. Send us a text message, they implored, and let us know what really goes on behind the scenes of a reality-TV show. Little did they know that all my mobiles, as well as my

Minidisc portable, my Psion netBook – in fact, all the things that help me get through the day – were about to be unceremoniously consfiscated for the week.

And what a hard day's week it was. Unfortunately for us, any idea of luxury hotels or off-camera fancy meals in restaurants was nonsense: the fact was that we were expected to endure this nightmare for a whole week. My fellow contestants were either he-men, anxious to dig holes in the bog with a spoon or hump fifty kilogrammes of stones across the desolate countryside, or he-women, possessed of great stamina and endurance, able to out-perform and outfox the men at most turns.

Then there was me: I can't light fires, dig holes, build tents, box-girder bridges, fashion windcheaters, or anything like that. I had not a clue what I had let myself in for. When it came down to it, it was quite shocking, leaving me dazed and bewildered for for the first couple of days.

Now this really was the stuff of *Around Ireland with a Pan:* all we had to last a week and to feed eight were a few battered pots, three carrots, half a dozen potatoes, a jar of peanut butter, sixteen Mars bars, porridge oats, some apples and oranges, the aforementioned bread (half a pan loaf) with yummy blue mould on it, and all the water (in the form of rain) a body could need. (In fact, it commenced raining the second the cameras began to roll and only ceased the moment the victor was declared.)

After watching my fellow contestants boil potatoes and carrots together (while rightly grumbling 'What's up with oul' super-chef here?'), what culinary sensibilities I possess began to return, and within a couple of days a few ideas came to me (helped by my fellow contestants using their noggins and gathering some exquisite and organic fresh mussels from the shore). In the meantime, helped by a bottle of whiskey which one of our number had managed to blag on board, I came up with the immortal breakfast idea which I baptised *flocons d'avoine en bouillie au whiskey irlandais et aux pepites de chocolat* – the wordy French title lending some sort of dignity to our morning ritual in the midst of the filth, the muck, the rain and the cold. Of course, all it was was porridge, rendered worthy of being a breakfast at the Ritz by the addition of Bushmills, Mars-bar shavings and, I almost forgot, some burnt orange peel, which, when infused, lends a warmth of flavour to the ensemble and combines deliciously with the whiskey. On the whole, it was really very good, though no doubt our appetites were sharpened by hunger and the aperitif of rain.

This in turn led to another idea, which was elegantly simple but put a smile on our crusty faces for a brief half-hour. Almost the same ingredients were fashioned into a wild apple crumble (it wan't that the apples were wild, just the conditions under which it was made). The trick here was to have the main part of the crumble in one pot and to use the base of another, made red-hot by placing it directly onto the fire, as a kind of elementary salamander. When put on top of the first pot containing the 'crumble', the heat grilled the improvised topping of porridge oats, mixed with carrot scrapings for their sugar, and toasted them to give the crumble effect. Well, sort of.

The crowning glory was probably the mussels, which I have to add were done properly for once as *moules marinières,* that is without cream, which is so often added in error in restaurant cooking. We, funnily enough, did not have any cream and so could not be accused of departing from the classic recipe as laid down in the *Repertoire de la Cuisine.* Quite where we managed to obtain an onion and a small bottle of dry white wine is anybody's guess: my lips shall remain sealed on that particular subject.

It has to be said that it was probably the best bowl of mussels I have enjoyed since my introduction to them on a beach at Etretat in Normandy many years ago. This time, lost in the pitch of the Mayo night, the sumptuousness of the dish wasn't down to any great culinary expertise on my part but rather to the plumpness and intensity of flavour of the wild mussels, the emptiness of our tums, and, it must be said, the camaraderie that ensued. It was like a Mayo *Babette's Feast* for eight celebrity C-list loonies. It could have done with some parsley and garlic, all the same.

Should you ever find yourself lost in the bog in Mayo with seven other mouths to feed and a multi-camera crew recording your every move, I hope these off-the-cuff recipes will come in handy. Remember that the recipes will work in any Irish bog: just add your own rain.

Oh, did I win? Of course not.

FLOCONS D'AVOINE EN BOUILLIE
AU WHISKEY IRLANDAIS ET AUX PEPITES DE CHOCOLAT

250g porridge oats
Glass of Irish whiskey
Mars bar
Orange peel

So you want to survive in the wilds of Mayo? Boil a pot of water on your fire (I have a sneaking suspicion that water will be freely available), then add the oats at one go and stir in. Easy-peasy so far. Place the orange peel on the end of a stick and shove into the fire until it begins to darken. Then add to the porridge mixture, along with the whiskey, and leave to simmer. Finally, run the blade of a knife (Come on! You've brought a knife, right?) along the edge of the Mars Bar and shave the chocolate into the porridge.

It's ready! Remove the orange peel, leaving only its delicate flavour behind, eat up your porridge and give praise and thanks to the Lord for being alive.

(Note to Irish speakers: while we nordies call porridge 'brachán', them other ones with their funny-speak call it 'leite'. You get used to it.)

Apples (as many as you have)
Porridge oats
Carrots
Any whiskey you haven't drunk yet

Luxury! This is a two-pot dish. Peel and dice your apples and place in the pot on the flame. Put the other, empty pot in the hottest part of the fire. (I'm afraid you don't have that much control over the heat of the flame, but it really doesn't matter.) If you can steal some butter, then do so and add it for that 'homely feeling'.

Using your 'Mars bar' knife, grate some carrots as finely as you can into the apples, for their natural sugar. Add the fudge part of the Mars bar, now that you've scraped off all the chocolate into that morning's porridge. (If you've eaten this bit, then tough!)

When the apples have reduced to a compote, add the whiskey. Then top this mixture with a layer of porridge oats and more carrot scrapings – if your wrist can take any more.

Place the empty pot into the pot containing your 'crumble' and listen excitedly while the red-hot bottom acts as a grill and toasts your oats.

Eat directly from the pot for unrestrained fun.

MOULES MARINIÈRES

Mussels (gathered in quantity on a beach, in the rain)
1 onion
Butter (yeah, right)
White wine
Parsley

In an ideal world, you would have all these ingredients in your kitchen, not in a County Mayo bog. But what is more important here is the cooking method. The action of just a little liquid (water or white wine) creates steam, killing the mussels and allowing them to release their natural juices, which creates the delicious broth that can be drunk after eating the mussels. This is why in so many restaurants you get a bowlful of mussels with more than 50 percent of them closed. Someone hasn't understood the principle: they have covered the mussels on the bottom layer with wine and the mussels have therefore been prevented from opening.

If you have onion, parsley and butter, then great – add them. Garlic is not part of the *'marinière'* recipe – though it is not unwelcome – but cream is redundant (even if there was a Fresh Cream Emporium open all hours in the pouring rain in the middle of the most user-hostile part of Mayo).

When the mussels have opened and are cooked, give them a good stir to mix your filched parsley and onions all the way through, and then eat as many as you can. Note that a knife and fork are never needed to eat mussels: eat the first one with your fingers and then use the empty shell to pluck out all the others. Do try this at home.

Eating is one of my favourite things; the other is listening to music. I'm surely never happier than when partnering the two of them, though it may surprise some to learn that I never played music in my restaurant, Shay Beano, since, although I felt that I had every right to force food down people's throats, and charge them for it, I never felt that I had the same right to impose my musical taste upon anyone in that setting. I had an idea that I was right when one of Ireland's leading musical luminaries, Christy Moore, one of my regular diners, said to me at the end of a meal: 'Thanks be to God you've no music here.'

In Ireland for many years we married music and music-making with a 'feed of pints' rather than food proper. Food was something that was endured later on, because the body demanded it: it got in the way of the tunes. Roscommon is one of those counties in which this older Ireland can still be glimpsed. There are of course some fine restaurants and country house dotted here and there, but the county is generally a place for great music, pints of plain, and plain food.

It was only when I was living in Brittany that I experienced the joys of food meeting music, in the form of a rollicking Irish session in a bar called Le Château inside the walls of Saint-Malo. We were still basically kids, and the owner let us play there without interference, just like in Ireland. We were also free to collect money if any was offered, and he would throw in the odd beer. More importantly, you could buy beer by the pitcher and ask for any number of glasses you wanted: it was around two francs per round cheaper that way. One day, in the midst of a mighty session, featuring Irish, Scots and Bretons, some of the leading musicians, the well-known Molard brothers from the town, just upped and, it seemed, left – to my chagrin. Happily, they returned half an hour later with baguettes, *bâtards* and *ficelles* (all types of French stick), patés, cheeses, hams, salamis, gherkins, hard-boiled eggs, tomatoes and *carottes rapées* (grated carrots). It was important to eat, they said: the food was paid for out of our earnings from the hat being passed around. We feasted between tunes and the session took off once more, the beer flying.

One of my favourite food and music stories is the tale of the great Jamaican guitarist Ernest Ranglin (whose music has supplied at least three of my radio and TV programmes with signature tunes), who has featured on a great many well-known Jamaican hits (he is the guitarist on 'My Boy Lollipop' from 1964) and who taught Bob Marley to play. Ernest was on tour in West Africa in 1975 as a member of the band backing Jimmy Cliff. While they were in Senegal, they spotted a fifteen-year-old Baaba Maal performing. The pair were convinced that the teenager would one day be a superstar.

In 1998, superstar Baaba Maal invited Ernest Ranglin and other Jamaican musicians to his home in Dakar to play music together. Every night they would all sit in Maal's kitchen to eat the national dish, fish and rice, with the left hand, as is customary, before repairing to the makeshift studio in his house at around midnight. There, they made powerful music, which was recorded on some ancient valve amps and acoustic microphones, giving the music an eerie, magical quality, resulting in the album *In Search of the Lost Riddim*, where lilting Jamaican rhythms meet the full, unplugged might of Sengalese *mbalax* music.

Watching the new *Planxty Live 2004* DVD, issued in the wake of the band's recent re-formation for a series of concerts, I was reminded of the importance of Roscommon to the band, given that they all used to convene in Grehan's pub in Boyle, to listen to other musicians and to play. It was there that they heard the great singer John Reilly. Much of his store of songs eventually made it into their repertoire: his influence greatly shaped their approach to music and helped turn Planxty into the supergroup that it became.

Of course, food plays some part in Planxty lore: the sleeve notes to *Prosperous*, the seminal 1972 album that acted as a catalyst for the band's formation proper, tells how they had 'made our way to my sister Anne's splendid sandwiches in her splendid kitchen in her splendid house at Prosperous, then down to the dungeons to make the record.' It was a very Irish approach to recording that has echoes of Ernest Ranglin's and Babba Maal's meeting – and procuced equally splendid results.

The funny thing is, thirty-odd years later it is Irish musicians who love their food and demand a bit more than 'splendid sandwiches'; I used to notice the sheer number of well-known names in Irish music who graced my dining room, more abundant than any other type of artist (except writers – hoping for inspiration out of that second bottle). I am sure that this is because our fabulous Irish music (the first really successful 'world' music) took its practitioners around the globe and exposed them to great food – particularly that of Brittany and other parts of France in the early period of the Irish trad revival

Imagine if, in today's Ireland, the session pubs, now free of choking smoke, could serve some great but simple Irish food along with the music, borrowing from our own traditon but adding to it, with nods to our Celtic neighbours, and influences culled from our visitors, much as we did with the music itself? I am delighted to offer two such fanciful recipes here in an effort to kick-start such notions.

I spent quite a bit of time in Turin, where the local cusine (Italian but greatly influenced by the Franco-Provençal region of which the Piedmont is part) was rustic, hearty – and an eternal source of not only pleasure but also ideas.

One evening after a particularly hearty dinner, we went off to a tavern where an Irish 'session' was promised. This turned out to be the case: only the *bodhrán* player was Irish, the rest were Italians – and all were more than competent in Irish music, having mastered several regional styles, as well as a vast store of jigs and reels.

I glanced up at a blackboard and spotted the evening special: risotto of rabbit with Guinness. This sounded unmissable. Despite my full belly, I ordered it, 'just to taste', you understand.

Risotto-making is a conundrum to most people as well as most restaurants. Many restaurants try to cheat by cooking the risotto only part-way and then finishing it off when it is ordered. This only works part of the time: a risotto ordered thus might be perfect at seven o'clock but will hardly be at half-past nine because, since it cannot be 'refreshed', it will continue to cook in its own heat.

No, risotto should be made to order. But while Italians are prepared to wait, Irish people aren't, and restaurateurs have had to come up with methods to speed up the service of same, with varying results.

It seems to me that this risotto is perfectly suited to Irish products and ingredients, and should feature prominently around the country. We have the rabbit, we have the Guinness, we only need to import the rice – which must be *arborio* or *carnaroli*, the latter of which is more expensive but is the king of rices.

1 packet *arborio* or *carnaroli* rice
1 onion
Olive oil
500ml chicken stock
1 young rabbit (jointed)

250g oyster mushrooms
1 bottle Guinness
1 bunch parsley
Parmesan cheese
Irish butter
Bay leaves
1 bunch of thyme

Making a risotto is not difficult, but it requires attention and patience, and must be served when ready – so don't start it until all your guests are in situ and have a drink in hand.

First, fry the rabbit joints in a little oil, browning them on all sides and leaving them to cook over a low heat while you prepare the risotto.

Dice the onion and fry it gently in a little olive oil with a few bay leaves. Do not allow it to brown. Add the rice, and fry this too a little in the oil. After a few minutes, add the stock, a little at a time, waiting until it has been absorbed before adding any more.

Add more stock and tear the oyster mushrooms apart and add them to the risotto, along with the thyme and the Guinness. The dish should begin to take on an attractive light-brown colour. Continue to stir and add stock as necessary.

Then add the rabbit pieces to allow them to cook in the heat of the rice. After fifteen minutes the rice should taste almost cooked and should be wet and malleable, but with every grain separate and visible.

Remove from the heat, add a generous knob of butter and grate Parmesan cheese finely into the risotto. This is the trick: the 'creaminess' of a risotto should come from its liquid plus cheese and butter; no cream is ever added. The risotto will continue to cook in its own heat.

Stir in the chopped parsley, grate a little more cheese on top and serve.

SLIGO

The good burghers of Sligo will forgive me, I hope, for saying on TV that my memory of their town was of a fairly grey, one-street place. Not so. It is of course a quite colourful, three-street town situated in a county that boasts remarkable, tourist-beckoning scenery.

County Sligo is of course 'Yeats Country': the poet is on record as having said that 'the place that has really influenced my life most is Sligo'. Perhaps the most pleasant way of getting to Sligo (apart from a long trip by road or a rickety, interminable trip by train) is by air. As the plane circles the tiny airport prior to landing, it is quite clear from the awe-inspiring sight of the sea, of Benbulben standing guard, and of the plains all around below, just why Yeats felt the way he did.

Visitors are attracted in their droves by the memory of and legacy of Yeats: the Summer School, Winter School and Yeats Festival are just some of the activities associated with the poet. If this is activity for the soul then, equally, the visitor would be well advised to take advantage of being in Sligo to take care of his or her body as well! *'Il faut soigner le corps pour que l'âme s'y plaise'* remarked St Francois de Sale. ('To look after the soul, you must first look after the body.') The way to do that, as shall be seen, could be through Sligo's plentiful healthy and organic foodstuffs, but in the meantime one might consider taking a Celtic traditional seaweed bath out at Strandhill.

Now me, I prefer to eat seaweed the odd time, but the therapeutic power of seaweed baths is well known. Traditionally, seaweed baths have been used to provide relief from the painful symptoms of rheumatism, arthritis and muscular back pains. The therapeutic power of the seaweed baths is attributed to the high concentration of iodine and trace minerals found naturally in seaweed and seawater. Celtic Seaweed Baths, situated in the new Maritime Centre at Strandhill, is the first bathhouse to open seven days a week, twelve months a year.

As for food, it's not yet a major factor in the life of Sligo town insofar as restaurants go, though things are constantly improving. Rather, the town is fast becoming known as a supplier of produce, particularly organic produce. While Sligo is not yet on a par with west Cork, the signs are that this aspect of the town will rapidly develop.

Sligo has many great food shops and suppliers. Cosgrove's on Market Square is a traditional-looking shop that is a veritable Aladdin's Cave of both old-fashioned and modern ingredients. When I visited there looking for ingredients for a dish, there was nothing they did not have. If anything was not clearly visible, a question to a member of the brown-coated staff quickly turned up the errant item.

Mary O'Donnell has been running Tír na nÓg, a pioneering natural-food shop on Grattan Street, for twenty-four years. The shop's principal focus has been on fresh organic fruit and vegetables, which they source mainly from the Leitrim Organic Centre or from Denis Healy's Organic Delights in Wicklow; Mary also stocks 'only the best' in Irish cheeses. They also marinate their own olives and stock organic eggs, which come from Anne Wilson, another Sligo pioneer. Anne's Roscarbon Organic Eggs used the first commercial flock in the country licenced by the Department of Agriculture, and she is now supplying health-food shops as well as one hotel, one B&B and one restaurant: 'ethical traders', as she herself describes them. Anne says that she has had a very positive reaction to her organic hens' eggs and that sales are buoyant, but happily the operation remains small – and beautiful.

As for eating out in Sligo, one could do worse than frequent the excellent and labyrinthine Bistro Bianconi's, known principally as a pizzeria – if one could get a table. It was an astonishing thing that, in the middle of a small Irish town like Sligo, a single establishment could be hopping, nay jumping, in the way that it was on the midweek and otherwise quiet evening when I went there. It seemed as though all of Sligo was there, with seaweed-bath partakers and busloads of Yeats Country tourists all clamouring for tables. Bianconi, y'see, sells new-wave designer pizze, and the smell and the menu decriptions are irresistible. We eventually got a table after waiting for forty-five minutes in the agreeable entrance area, where one can sit or stand around small bar tables partaking of Peroni riserva beer or Chianti from the excellent wine menu. That memory alone is clear; what isn't quite so clear, such was the potency of the Chianti, is how good the pizze were when we eventually got to feast upon them. I do remember, though, that mine had artichokes (always as good sign) and that a great time was had by all (also a good sign).

Lately too, I have been hearing very favourable reports about the Atrium, located within the confines of the Nyland Gallery in Stephen Street. This restaurant is run by Bríd Torrades, who formerly ran the much-respected Glebe House just outside the town, and Our Hero Roy of 'Tá Sé Mahogany Gaspipes' fame. Roy also ran a much-loved Graeco-North African basement place – whose name escapes me – in D'Olier Street many years ago, at a time when Maghrebi cuisine was neither profitable nor popular. Roy, at the time of writing, has finally retired. The Atrium is, as befits Sligo, a simple little place specialising in local ingredients – and excellent ones from afar, where appropriate – witness the daily delivery of fine croissants from La Maison des Gourmets in Dublin. A blackboard menu, which changes daily, offers superb salads, sandwiches worthy of the name, and exquisite cakes.

As if this wasn't enough, check out Kate's Kitchen on Castle Street. Described as a 'twinshop', it is much more than that, selling rare-breed toiletries as well as the very best in delicatessen products and specialist foods. Their website is well worth a visit too (details below).

Donaghy's at Coach Lane is another marvellous Sligo near-institution, run by the indefatigable Andy Donaghy and his wife, Orla. A traditional bar downstairs gives way, upstairs, to cutting-edge food that has garnered a slew of awards; there are plenty of daring items on the international menu – Andy will readily serve up such esoteric items as catfish – as well as sure-footed crowd-pleasers like chicken wings.

Despite such a lengthy menu, I would have difficulty in straying from the very first item, foie gras, as is my wont. Equally, from a choice of meats and fish that must surely satisfy everyone, there is one item that stands out and for which I would return – by air, train or even (shudder) car – and that is the veal chop. I love veal chop. I crave veal chop. On my first visit to New York, I walked the streets all of my first morning there, not to see the sights but to find a proper Italian restaurant serving a proper veal chop. Andy does it in classic fashion – correctly cooked, medium rare – with Madeira and demi-glaze, but then turns it on its head with the addition of those lovely blue-stemmed mushrooms plus a cheeky hint of thyme. Clever lad, our Andy.

Finally, Sligo has also been home to many people who have chosen to come and live in Ireland from mainly Continental countries in the last twenty to thirty years, in search of a self-sufficient lifestyle. For some time now, we have seen the rewards of that influence – in the form of the incredible incidence of organic foodstuffs and health-food shops dotted around the town and environs.

Volkmar Klohn is one such who came to this country nearly a dozen years ago. Originally, he produced raw milk cheese but – as with so many others in the business – he became disenchanted with this business, owing to the extremely strict application of EU food regulations in Ireland, and turned his hand to fresh vegetables and organic herbs instead. His excellent and delicious produce can be bought at Tír na nÓg and sampled in Andy Donaghy's Coach Lane restaurant.

CHAR-GRILLED LOIN VEAL CHOP WITH WOOD-GROWN PIED-BLUE ORGANIC MUSHROOMS AND INFUSED THYME FLOWER OIL

4 eight-to-ten-ounce milk-fed veal chops
    (fillets attached if possible)
4 to 6 ounces of pied-blue (or similar organic)
    mushrooms
8 small shallots, left whole
1 clove of garlic, left whole
4 ounces of leeks, sliced
A good pinch of rock salt
Fresh cracked peppercorns
Thyme-flower oil (see below)
Reduced veal stock or good chicken stock
    (available in good delicatessens)
Eight-to-ten-year-old Madeira (the older the better)

for the thyme-flower oil:
1 cup of good-quality extra-virgin olive oil
A handful of thyme flowers

for the thyme-flower oil:
Heat the oil slightly with the thyme and a pinch of salt. Let it infuse overnight. Add half of it to the reduced veal stock and blend well.

for the veal:
Crank up the barbecue to maximum heat or, if you have one of those stoves with the grill on top, bring it up to 350°C. Salt and pepper your chops and rub with some of the infused oil. Place on the hot grill for two minutes each side. Set aside.

for the sauce:
Lightly sauté the whole garlic clove, shallots and pied-blue mushrooms in a knob of butter. When ready, deglaze the pan with a large shot of Madeira, then add about one cup of the veal stock.

Reduce for three or four minutes until the sauce starts to thicken slightly. Remove from the heat and add one tablespoon of butter, moving it around the sauce until it dissolves. This will give the sauce a rich, shiny consistency. Discard the whole clove of garlic.

to serve:
Spoon the sauce in equal amounts on to four plates, place the veal chops back on the grill and heat for thirty seconds. When hot, remove and place on top of the sauce. Add a drizzle of thyme oil and a sprig of thyme to garnish.

New boiled potatoes in June, skin on, with minted butter, are the perfect addition on the side. Sit down and enjoy this with some friends and a bottle, or two, of Pinot noir.

I was staying in the tiny village of Kinlough, population two to three hundred. The cut of the village, not far from Ballyshannon and the border with Donegal, did not offer me succour in my dwindling hope that anything, other than the comforting boxty for which Leitrim is famous, could be found to eat. This then is the real Ireland, I thought, far from the safety nets of Dublin, Belfast, Cork and Galway, their trendy bistros, their wine bars dispensing glasses of Monsieur Roederer's finest. You're stuck, Éamonn, I thought to myself, stuck without a paddle, or even a shop selling paddles, and if it rains much more, you're going to need one, big-time.

Seen from somewhere like Belfast, the popular image of Leitrim is that of a barren county, the endless subject of articles on *Nationwide* and other such current-affairs programmes about the people leaving the land and of government attempts to repopulate it. It was therefore with some trepidation that I went off to spend a long weekend in the county. True to form, it initially lived up to its reputation, raining constantly. Why have I just written 'initially'? As an attempt to soften the blow? Tell the bloody truth: it rained non-stop for the entire time I was there. It rained on my parade, it bucketed on my barbecue, and it drenched my dill mayonnaise.

Don't mind the rain: I could not have been more wrong about the village and what might be found to eat therein. I was delighted to be so completely, utterly wrong. Kinlough is host to a charming guesthouse and a fabulous restaurant called the Courthouse (which, not surprisingly, used to be the local courthouse) run by an impish chap called Piero Melis from Sardinia and his wife, Sandra. Piero has been in Ireland for some eight years now and offers accommodation in four splendidly appointed rooms. Indeed, he has just been listed in *The Bridgestone Irish Food Guide* as one of the top hundred places to stay in Ireland.

In case I didn't mention it, there is also a fabulous restaurant. If I did, I'm mentioning it again. The cooking is an Italian-

Mediterranean and Irish hybrid; slowly but surely, as the Irish market develops and changes, Piero is introducing more and more dishes from his island homeland.

When we ate there on that wet weekend, the food was a total revelation, a meal of sheer quality from beginning to end and one that brought winning smiles to the faces of all concerned. The prices were honest, and quite a revelation compared to similar establishments in Dublin.

The current menu keeps many of the crowd-pleasing dishes intact: a simple dish of grilled fillet of beef was one of the best I have ever tasted – succulent and toothsome, confidently sauced, and cooked not just to perfection but also as requested. Mouth-watering modern Italian dishes have been added to the menus, however. Among these are turbot and squid-ink risotto with *bottarga*. The latter is grated dried tuna roe, a Sardinian caviar if you will, which is ruddy in colour and adds a subtle and mellow undertone to the thrust of the squid ink. Incidentally, *bottarga* is also excellent when partnered with spaghetti.

The real star of the show has to be the smoked-swordfish carpaccio. Although this was a new one on me, I had been introduced to smoked tuna while on a 2002 visit to France and had found it quite exquisite. The swordfish is similar but responds even better to the smoking than the tuna, bringing out a length of flavour from this most noble of fish, which, should it suffer cooking at all, ought really only to be breathed on by angels. Piero brings the smoked swordfish in directly from Sardinia; this dish alone would make the trip from anywhere in Ireland to Kinlough worth it.

Meat-lovers will enjoy the restaurant's veal dish – escalopes of veal rolled as *involtini* and stuffed with mozzarella, Parma ham and sage, the latter herb a nod to the classic *saltimbocca* of Rome. Again, Piero partners it with a risotto, this time a wild-mushroom one. For those of you who have ever suffered the texture of a poorly realised risotto, the Courthouse is the place to renew your acquaintance with this, the king of rice dishes.

Pastas are a little more pedestrian than the delights above, but do not think that they are any less delicious: try the brilliantly executed ricotta-and-spinach-stuffed ravioli with a tomato-and-basil sauce – a dish after my own stomach – and seafood fettuccine. The prosaic title of the latter does not give a hint as to the delights contained within: suffice to say that it is crammed full of the finest fish, the most plump and juicy shellfish, beautifully cooked pasta, and a white-wine-and-saffron sauce to die for (or indeed to kill anyone who stands in your way for).

Like so many of today's restaurateurs in Ireland, Piero pursues a policy of using local and national products wherever possible: duck from Turnhill, ostrich from Cork, fish and shellfish from Killybegs, and vegetables sourced from the splendid Organic Centre in Rossinver.

Piero's wine list too is exemplary, with many of the wines imported directly from Sardinia. Among them are numerous organic whites, which are now enjoying huge popularity among his regular customers, and the superb and justly famous Sardinian red, Turriga. Turriga is a big and intense wine, a serious wine, which was voted one of the best Italian wines of the past five years. It is made from 85 percent Cannonau, and 15 percent Malvasia Nera, Carignano and Bovale Sardo. The first vintage was bottled in 1988, and forty thousand bottles are produced annually. Along the way it has garnered Italy's coveted 'Tre Bicchieri' award from the prestigious Gambero Rosso guide.

With such impressive bottles on his list, it was a natural enough step for Piero to introduce wine-tastings at the Courthouse in May 2004, inviting the wine-makers over from Sicily to give tutored tastings. It is hoped that these will become a regular occurrence.

Punters are making the trip to the Courthouse's door from all over Ireland: there are easy links from Belfast and the rest of the north via Enniskillen, while more local regulars flock from Sligo, Manorhamilton and Bundoran. This is one of Ireland's truly hidden jewels and should not be missed.

North Leitrim is home too to the Organic Centre at Rossinver, just up the road from Kinlough. The centre is a non-profit-making organisation set in nineteen acres of beautiful countryside and within easy reach of Ballyshannon, Sligo and Donegal town. The centre has the aim of providing training, information and demonstrations of organic gardening, growing and farming. It provides a wide range of training courses for everyone from the enthusiastic amateur to the professional grower and boasts many demonstration gardens for visitors to admire. The centre has a vast array of training courses throughout the year and is a must for any visitor with an interest in organic methods and quality vegetables and herbs: see the gardens, drop into the café, or buy at the excellent on-site shop.

Finally, the legendary boxty justifies its legend and really should gain wider currency as one of Ireland's great culinary inventions. This dish is essentially a potato pancake of shredded and mashed potato and lends itself to a variety of interpretations. I have pleasure in offering my take on this Irish galette below, as well as the pasta dish I created in Piero's immaculate kitchen – with a little help from his perfect pesto.

Them that knows say that boxty is best eaten sitting beside a turf fire, but me, I think it's never better than when you're standing outside, soaked to the skin on one of those memorable days during the short-lived rainy season between January and December in Leitrim.

Boxty on the griddle, boxty in the pan,
If you can't make boxty, you'll never get your man.

BOXTY

Boxty is a traditional potato dish commonly eaten in the border counties. It is well suited to a variety of interpretations, some of which you can sample at the Boxty House in Dublin's Temple Bar. This quintessentially Irish dish would respond very well to our best products, such as smoked salmon – and would also have been an ideal base for this 'Paddy pizza', which I used to do years ago (at the time, with soda bread) in the McCausland Hotel in Belfast. This is the recipe that was demonstrated for me by traditional boxty-makers:

250g raw potato
250g mashed potato
250g plain flour
1 teaspoon baking powder
1 teaspoon salt
1 large knob of butter
125ml milk

to accompany:
Sausages
Rashers
Black pudding
White pudding
Tomatoes, thickly sliced
Eggs

First, grate the raw potatoes into a bowl using a cheese grater. When this is done, wring them in a cloth to extract the starchy liquid, then mix them thoroughly with the mashed potato. Melt the butter and mix this into the potatoes with the flour and baking powder, finally adding sufficient milk to form a dough. Spread out onto a dry, floured surface and knead the mixture well before cutting roughly four round, crêpe-like shapes of dough. Cook these on a hot griddle or heavy-based frying pan, turning once.

Meanwhile, cook the sausages, rashers, puddings and tomatoes in a pan. Fry the eggs in the fat. Slice the sausages and puddings, and cut up the rashers. Place the cooked boxty on a plate, top with the tomatoes, then pile on the other ingredients. Finally, add the fried egg. (A tip for frying eggs without turning them: splash a few drops of vinegar on the white immediately around the yolk, to 'cook' it.)

Do not put pesto or mozzarella anywhere near it!

When I was in Piero's kitchen I found the most excellent pesto, which I used in the following dish. This dish features green beans and thin slices of potatoes and goat's cheese. It's a tasty number, easy to prepare and ideal for vegetarians and passing American presidents. (I once served it to a former Leader of the Western World who popped up from the American Embassy with three carloads of haircuts and very dark shades in tow to the RDS, where I was cooking at the time, and ordered it. Trouble was, he ordered a goat's-cheese salad as a starter, then called for this main course featuring the same goat's cheese halfway though, and then, without batting an eyelid, asked for a salad to go with it!)

Fazzoletti, incidentally, could be described as an 'open lasagne'. The word means 'handkerchief' and refers to the way the top layer of pasta is placed on top of the ingredients. A good-quality artisanal pasta is perfect for this dish, but if you want to make your own, use Barry Smith's recipe for pasta on page 64.

8 sheets of good-quality lasagne
1 slice of goat's-cheese log per person
1 courgette, diced
100g fine green beans
1 red chilli, deseeded and chopped
2 red peppers, roughly chopped
Fresh parsley
3 tomatoes
Salt and pepper
Olive oil
Cayenne pepper

for the pesto:
Loads of basil
    (the sauce will keep, so make plenty at the one go)
100g pine kernels
150g grated Parmesan cheese
4 cloves of garlic

Salt and pepper
Extra-virgin olive oil

Serves 4

for the pesto:
Place the garlic, pine kernels and Parmesan in a food blender and pulse them repeatedly until you obtain a coarse mixture. Then add all of the basil and pulse again repeatedly. Add about 250ml of olive oil and blend until you have a thick paste. Add more if necessary, but keep the pesto quite thick. Transfer to one or more jars, seal and keep in the fridge.

for the fazzoletti:
Season the courgette, peppers and chilli and fry them together in a little olive oil. Blanch the green beans for one minute in lightly salted boiling water and then refresh them under cold water. Cut them up in small pieces and add to the pan. Dice the tomatoes and keep to one side.

Cook the sheets of lasagne in a large pot of boiling water. (It may be preferable to cook them in two lots. By the way, putting oil in the water to stop them sticking is a nonsense: it just floats to the top.) Cook for about five minutes or until ready. Strain and apply olive oil to them immediately for flavour, and to prevent them sticking together while you assemble the dish. Dust the cheese rounds with cayenne pepper and drizzle lightly with olive oil. Place under the grill for about four minutes.

Place one sheet of lasagne flat on each of four warm plates and add some pesto to each sheet. Spoon on some of the courgette mixture, give a final twist of black pepper and spoon some pesto on top. Place the by-now-browned slices of goat's cheese on each portion of the mixture. Finally, add the top sheet of pasta, crumpling it as you put it on so that it resembles a hankie – and does not obscure the filling underneath. Place some pesto on top. Season with more black pepper, scatter with the diced tomatoes and place a sprig of basil on each serving. Call the White House and tell him supper's ready.

DIRECTORY

FERMANAGH
O'Doherty's Fine Meats
Belmore Street, Enniskillen, County Fermanagh
Tel from ROI: 048 6632 2152
from NI: 028 6632 2152
Email: sales@blackbacon.com

Oscar's Restaurant
28 Belmore Street, Enniskillen
Tel from ROI: 0488 6632 7037
from NI: 028 6632 7037

DERRY
Beech Hill Country House Hotel
32 Ardmore Road, Derry City
Tel from ROI: 048 7134 9279
from NI: 028 7134 9279

Browne's Bar and Brasserie
1-2 Bonds Hill, Derry
Tel from ROI: 048 7134 5180
from NI: 028 7134 5180

Exchange Restautant and Wine Bar
Queens Quay, Derry
Tel from ROI: 048 7127 3990
from NI: 028 7127 3990

An Bacús
34 Upper Great James Street, Derry
Tel from ROI: 048 7126 4678
from NI: 028 7126 4678

ANTRIM
Walter Ewing
124 Shankill Road, Belfast
Tel from ROI: 048 9032 5534
from NI: 028 9032 5534

Sawers
7B Fountain Centre, College Street, Belfast
Tel from ROI: 048 9032 2021
from NI: 028 9032 2021

Cayenne
7 Ascot House, Shaftesbury Square, Belfast
Tel from ROI: 048 9033 1532
from NI: 028 9033 1532

Zen
55-59 Adelaide Street, Belfast
Tel from ROI: 048 9023 2244
from NI: 028 9023 2244

Deane's Brasserie
38-40 Howard Street, Belfast
Tel from ROI: 048 9056 0000
from NI: 028 9056 0000
www.deanesbelfast.com

Chokdee
44 Bedford Street, Belfast
Tel from ROI: 048 9024 8800
from NI: 028 9024 8800

James Street South Restaurant
21 James Street South, Belfast
Tel from ROI: 048 9043 4310
from NI: 028 9043 4310
www.jamesstreetsouth.co.uk

H20
Kingsway Centre, Dunmurry
Tel from ROI: 048 9030 9000
from NI: 028 9030 9000

DOWN
Shanks
The Blackwood, Crawfordsburn Road, Bangor
Tel from ROI: 048 9185 3313
from NI: 028 9185 3313
www.shanksresatuarant.com

The Buck's Head
77 Main Street, Dundrum
Tel from ROI: 048 4375 1868
from NI: 028 4375 1868

James Nicholson Wine Merchant
27A Killyleagh Street, Crossgar,
Downpatrick
Tel from ROI: 048 4483 0091
from NI: 028 4483 0091
Email: info@jnwine.com
www.jnwine.com

Oriel
2 Bridge Street, Gilford,
Tel from ROI: 048 83 1543
from NI: 028 3883 1543

ARMAGH
The Seagoe Hotel
Upper Church Lane, Portadown
Tel from ROI: 048 38 333 076
from NI: 028 38 333 076

The Famous Grouse
16 Ballyhagen Road, Loughgall
Tel from ROI: 048 38 891 778
from NI: 028 38 891 778

Moyallon Foods
76 Crowhill Road, Craigavon
Tel from ROI: 048 38 349 100
from NI: 028 38 349 100

MONAGHAN
Castle Leslie
Glaslough
Tel: 047 88109
email: info@castleleslie.com

CAVAN
MacNean Bistro
Blacklion
Tel: 072 53022

MEATH
The Station House Hotel
Kilmessan
Tel: 046 902 5239
Email:info@thestationhousehotel.com

WESTMEATH
Wineport Lodge
Glasson, Athlone
Tel: 090 643 9010

Wines Direct Ireland Ltd
Irishtown, Mullingar
Tel: 0444 0634
Email: paddykeogh@wines-direct.com

LONGFORD
Torc Truffles Ltd
Athlone Road, Longford
Tel: 043 47353
Email: info@torctruffles.ie

OFFALY
Spinners Townhouse and Bistro
Castle Street, Birr
Tel: 0509 21673

Prue & David Rudd & Family Ltd
Syngefield Industrial Estate, Kinnitty
Road, Birr
Tel: 0509 22508

LAOIS
The Kingfisher Restaurant
Old AIB Bank, Portlaoise
Tel: 0502 62500

KILDARE
The K Club
Straffan
Tel: 01 601 7200
Email: resortsales@kclub.ie

Moyglare Manor Hotel
Maynooth
Tel: 01 628 6351

Les Olives
10 South Main Street, Naas
Tel: 045 894 788

Osprey
Devoy Quarter, Naas
Tel: 045 881 111
Email: info@osprey.ie

DUBLIN
Nicos Restaurant
53 Dame Street, Dublin 2
Tel: 01 677 3062

Ar Vicoletto Osteria Romano
5 Crowe Street, Dublin 2
Tel: 01 670 8662

The Old Mill
14 Temple Bar, Dublin 2
Tel: 01 671 9262 / 01 679 6602

The Tea Room
The Clarence Hotel, 6-8 Wellington
Quay, Dublin 2.
Tel: 01 670 9000

Les Frères Jacques
74 Dame Street, Dublin 2
Tel: 01 679 4555

Havana
3 Camden Market, Grantham Street,
Dublin 8
Tel: 01 476 0046
Email: info@havana.ie

The Ely Wine Bar
22 Ely Place, Dublin 2
Tel: 01 676 8986

Peploe's Wine Bistro
16 St Stephen's Green, Dublin 2
Tel: 01 676 3144
www.peploes.com

KILKENNY
Zuni
26 Patrick Street, Kilkenny
Tel: 056 772 3999
Email: info@zuni.ie
www.zuni.ie

WATERFORD
The Tannery
10 Quay Street, Dungarvan
Tel: 058 454 20
Web: www.tannery.ie

TIPPERARY
The Cherry Tree
Lakeside, Ballina, Killaloe
Tel: 061 375 688

CORK
Café Paradiso
16 Lancaster Quay, Cork
Tel: 021 427 7939

Ivory Tower
The Exchange Buildings, Princes
Street, Cork
Tel: 021 427 4665

Fishy Fishy Café
The Guardwell, Kinsale
Tel: 021 477 4453

KERRY
Fenton's
Green Street, Dingle
Tel: 066 915 2172

Beginish Restaurant
Green Street, Dingle
Tel: 066 915 1588

GALWAY
Nimmo's
Spanish Arch, Galway
Tel: 091 561 114

Le Blason
Main Street, Oughterard
Tel: 091 557111

Pierre's Restaurant
8 Quay Street, Galway city
Tel: 091 566 066
Email: kirwans@indigo.ie

Viña Mara
19 Middle Street, Galway city
Tel: 091 561 610
Email: vinamara@hotmail.com

SLIGO
Carraig Fhada Seaweeds
Frank Melvin Sea Vegetable Products,
Cabra, Rathlee, Easkey
Tel: 096 49042

Cosgrove's
Market Square
Tel: 0719 142 809

Tír na nÓg
Grattan Street
Tel: 071 62752

Bistro Bianconi's
44 O'Connell Street
Tel: 071 41744

The Atrium
Model Arts and Niland Gallery, The
Mall, Sligo town
Tel: 071 914 1418

Kate's Kitchen
3 Castle Street, Sligo town
Tel: 0719 143 022
www.kateskitchensligo.com

LEITRIM
The Courthouse
Kinlough
Tel: 072 42391

The Organic Centre
Rossinver
Tel: 071 985 4338

Index of Recipes

penne
pennette with broccoli, pine kernels
and chilli   32
ravioli
ravioli of wild mushrooms and black
bacon   24
spaghettini
spaghettini with Walter Ewing's
smoked salmon and dulse   48
spaghettini alle vongole   207
tagliatelle
tagliatelle with grilled chicken, charred
peppers and cream   30

peppercorns, green
roast loin of organic pork with a sauce
of Black Bush, wild Irish honey and
green peppercorns   52

peppers, sweet
tagliatelle with grilled chicken, charred
peppers and cream   30

pesto   244

pine kernels
pennette with broccoli, pine kernels
and chilli   32

pork
roast loin of organic pork with a sauce
of Black Bush, wild Irish honey and
green peppercorns   52

braised belly of Ulster pork, creamed
savoy cabbage, shallot purée and sherry-vinegar glaze   61
Thai roast-pork salad   69

porridge
flocons d'avoine en bouillie au
whiskey irlandais et aux pepites de
chocolat   224

potatoes
hachis Parmentier   81
potato apple   103
Rudd's bacon chops with mashed
potato, mustard cabbage and shallot
vinaigrette   107
omelette Parmentière   157
boxty   242

prunes
roast breast of turkey with prunes,
chestnut and Armagnac stuffing   89

quiche
nettle quiche   17

rabbit
risotto of rabbit with Guinness   230

raspberries
crème brûlée with raspberry tuiles 200

Ricard
snails with linguini, apple crisps and
Ricard cream   71

rice
chicken fried rice   180

risotto
courgette and broad-bean risotto with
tomato, mozzarella and basil   169
risotto of rabbit with Guinness   230

rogan josh   54

sage
tortino   159

salmon, smoked
spaghettini with Walter Ewing's
smoked salmon and dulse   48

sauce chien   111

254